"These survivors hit their mark in helping to change the conversation about borderline personality disorder (BPD), from one of fear and misunderstanding to one of empathy, evidence-based treatment, and hope. BPD is a relatively new DSM diagnosis with a ten percent suicide rate—and relatively new evidence-based treatments. Studies show that nearly forty percent of individuals diagnosed with bipolar disorder in fact have BPD, as the editors note. These BPD survivors describe more stable, less chaotic lives, as well as pure gratitude for the mental health professionals who diagnosed their BPD and provided either evidence-based treatment or otherwise compassionate and committed care."

—**Jim Payne**, former president of the
National Alliance on Mental Illness

"Saying that these are important stories is not enough. These are essential stories, to be read and digested by anyone with BPD, anyone who has a loved one with BPD, and any professionals (not just mental health professionals) who work with people with BPD. These wonderful and courageous authors help us understand their suffering, and then show us how they created hope, and a life worth living, from the depths of despair. This is truly an educational and inspirational book."

—**Alan E. Fruzzetti, PhD**, professor and director of
dialectical behavior therapy (DBT) and research
program department of psychology at the University
of Nevada, Reno

"This compelling book grasps the tragedy and suffering of BPD in a way that I hope will reduce some of the stigma of the disorder. I am quite happy to see they have included stories of people finding their way out of hell. It is important to appreciate that once in hell, it is possible to climb out of it."

—**Marsha Linehan, PhD, ABPP**, developer of dialectical behavior therapy (DBT)

BEYOND BORDERLINE

TRUE STORIES OF RECOVERY FROM BORDERLINE PERSONALITY DISORDER

EDITED BY
JOHN G. GUNDERSON, MD
PERRY D. HOFFMAN, PHD

New Harbinger Publications, Inc.

Publisher's Note

This publication is designed to provide accurate and authoritative information in regard to the subject matter covered. It is sold with the understanding that the publisher is not engaged in rendering psychological, financial, legal, or other professional services. If expert assistance or counseling is needed, the services of a competent professional should be sought.

Distributed in Canada by Raincoast Books

Copyright © 2016 by John G. Gunderson and Perry D. Hoffman
          New Harbinger Publications, Inc.
          5674 Shattuck Avenue
          Oakland, CA 94609
          www.newharbinger.com

Cover design by Amy Shoup; Interior design by Michele Waters-Kermes; Acquired by Melissa Valentine; Edited by Brady Kahn

---

Library of Congress Cataloging-in-Publication Data

TK

18   17   16

10   9   8   7   6   5   4   3   2   1   First Printing

Contents

Foreword
by Brandon Marshall

For five years my life was a living hell. I had no clue what was going on. I spent years talking to doctors—sometimes three or four in one week. It wasn't until I received the diagnosis of borderline personality disorder that I was able to grab hold of my life. People only saw what was unfolding on ESPN—the DUI arrest, the domestic disputes—that was the story the public was absorbing. What they didn't see—couldn't possibly know—was the days I sat in a dark room, the days that went by when I didn't utter a single word, and the persistent game of dramatic emotional changes that was going on inside me.

When I got the diagnosis I immediately felt better. I understood, I could *be* understood, and I could be treated. After doing the work, I earned my life back.

At McLean Hospital I decided to tell my story to the world. I had millions of people at my disposal through my platform— millions would hear my story. Maybe it was impulsivity that made me decide to go public. Dr. Gunderson sat me down and explained how vulnerable I would make myself. He talked about how the announcement would publicly magnify my symptoms and life. To be honest, he wasn't thrilled about my plan. He wanted to be certain I was ready. In any event, I am glad I followed this path, and I also greatly admire those who have decided to tell their stories in this book. I expect it was liberating for them just as it was for me. I look forward to a time when others will go public about their trials and hopefully with their triumphs with this trying disorder. The louder our voices, the more we will be heard. BPD is treatable, and people do not need to stay in the mental health system forever, unlike many other diagnoses.

My time at McLean Hospital presented me with some of the most phenomenally challenging experiences of my life thus far. Taking my life back meant losing what I thought was the most important part of me—the fabric of my being, the things that made up the football player that I had been my whole life. I can never explain the feeling I felt when we got to the root of my issues with anger and fears of abandonment. I can still remember uncovering those issues like it was yesterday. There were so many times I found myself sitting in Dr. Gunderson's office, my eyes welling with tears. The realization —the spark—revealed a heart filled with anger, pain, resentment, and sadness. My heart. The waves of emotion were profound and liberating.

I always tell people that while at McLean Hospital I discovered what life was really about. I didn't get my old life back. When I left, I was a totally different person. My eyes opened up to allow me to be my better self—a different person. I understood what I was feeling. I learned to validate those feelings and those of others. I also learned how to talk about those feelings. When I read the stories in this book, those memories return and I feel deeply for my fellow patients with BPD. This time it is not the feelings of anger and fear that tormented me when I began my recovery; it is feelings of sympathy and hope that I had not known before.

I left with the tools to cope and manage it all. I realized that the fight wasn't over, but I was and remain confident that I have the tools and skills to manage life's challenges so I can have a healthy and effective life.

Looking back now, I know the most impactful part of all of the time I spent at McLean happened in the first week I was there. I was invited to a workshop comprised of doctors, clinicians, and patients. The most powerful voices of all were those of the patients.

Their stories gave me hope. This wonderful collection of stories by people with BPD who are in the process of recovery offers the same powerful message of hope to the many others whose BPD is untreated or is, too often, still not diagnosed.

I hope readers will join me in advocating for better awareness, and better treatment for those suffering as I have from borderline personality disorder. In hope, life springs back, and for me a purpose beyond football and family was laid before me. All of the patients in this book, and its readers, are now a part of that purpose.

Introduction

Seldom does an illness, medical or psychiatric, carry such intense stigma and deep shame that its name is whispered, or a euphemism coined, and its sufferers despised and even feared.

Perhaps leprosy or syphilis or AIDS fits this category.

Borderline personality disorder (BPD) is such an illness. In fact, it has been called the "leprosy of mental illnesses" and the disorder with "surplus stigma." It may actually be the most misunderstood psychiatric disorder of our age.

Perhaps the greatest instigators of BPD's stigma have been psychiatrists, psychologists, and social workers. For many years, clinicians spoke and wrote in pejorative terms about patients diagnosed with the disorder as "the bane of my existence," "a run for my money," "exhausting," or "treatment rejecting." In fact, professionals have often declined to work with people diagnosed with BPD. This rejection by professionals, which has seemed at times almost phobic, has spanned many decades. Patients with tendencies toward self-injury, suicide threats, and suicide attempts have been described in the literature as manipulative, treatment resistant, raging, or malignant. A causal connection between too much exposure to BPD patients and professional burnout has been commonly assumed.

Outside clinical circles, the term *borderline personality disorder* itself, connoting people bordering on psychosis, with fatally flawed personalities, has promoted the stigma. Characterizations in movies, notably Alex, Glenn Close's character in *Fatal Attraction,* and Susanna, played by Winona Ryder in *Girl, Interrupted,* have nurtured the popular conception of those with BPD as evil, dangerous, and destructive or as selfish, manipulative, and noncompliant. These characterizations—especially Alex, who comes across in the end as a horror-film monster—offer little nuance or positivity, but rather are depictions of people to steer clear of.

For most people, the reality of BPD is a mystery. Here are some facts. Borderline personality disorder is a serious, often misunderstood mental illness characterized by pervasive instability in moods, interpersonal relationships, self-image, and behavior. It is a disorder of emotional dysregulation. This instability often disrupts family and work, long-term planning, and the individual's sense of identity.

The prevalence of BPD in the general population is evenly split between the genders, though women present for treatment far more often than men. More than fourteen million Americans have the disorder, making it more common than bipolar disorder (manic-depressive illness) and schizophrenia, combined. BPD patients are often misdiagnosed; for example, nearly 40 percent of people diagnosed as bipolar are, in fact, borderline. There is a heritability factor of about 67 percent. Interestingly, it is one of the few psychiatric illnesses that is not lifelong, with remission likely and relapses rare.

Since the symptoms of BPD are most vividly evident in the context of relationships, the disorder always directly and personally impacts the lives of others. Both sufferers and their loved ones confront intimidating daily challenges, and the toll for everyone can be devastating.

Fortunately, considerable progress in treating BPD has been made in the past two decades. Several evidence-based treatments have emerged, changing lives and altering the futures of many sufferers. These treatments—Dr. Marsha Linehan's dialectical behavior therapy (DBT), doctors Anthony Bateman and Peter Fonagy's mentalization based therapy (MBT), Dr. Otto Kernberg's transference focused psychotherapy (TFP), and, most recently, coeditor Dr. John Gunderson's good psychiatric management (GPM)—and related research offer hope to sufferers and therapists alike. A diagnosis once met with universal pessimism is now being approached with much more optimism and with a willingness to reject the myth of BPD as an untreatable disorder.

This book of personal journeys offers a wider lens into the disorder, as people diagnosed with BPD share their struggles and successes. These accounts give us the opportunity to imagine ourselves in the shoes of people with BPD, helping us understand their lived experience in all its pain and triumph. Healing victories can come with successful treatment, and although each person's story is unique, they carry common threads of hope and courage.

We, the editors, have over eighty years of combined experience treating individuals with BPD and their families. We selected these stories from numerous submissions, seeking out those that reflect the variations in the course of the disorder and the individuality of each patient's struggles. We hope you will share our appreciation for the honesty and vulnerability of these stories, collected here in the service of combating the myths surrounding this diagnosis. We are very grateful to the authors, all of them brave people who took a risk in sharing their truths. Real names and other story details have been changed to protect anonymity.

Sometimes an illness, whether medical or psychiatric, progresses from hopeless untreatability to a trajectory of healing, resilience, and recovery. We believe BPD fits this category.

1. Anguish Management

An eerie silence allowed my cries of terror to fill the halls, a surge of despair rushing through my core as I pleaded for release. The antiseptic smell coated my nostrils with each gasp for breath. No soft touch comforted me. No reassuring voice consoled me. My body pressed up against the locked door within the confines of an institution, a consequence of my desperate attempts to manage my shattered and crippling existence. It was here I found myself alone in a horror movie.

I often felt secluded, even in the presence of others. I was unable to relate to my peers, to my family, or even to myself. I struggled with the idea of self-awareness, a consistent identity an elusive concept. I looked more like a boy than the girl I was, my toys reflecting my confusion. Cars and trucks lined my toy box along with a few dolls, most with hair cut to the scalp. When I would play with them, it was far from the typical loving display of a child mimicking her mother. I remember sitting on the cold floor in the basement playroom, little more inviting than a dingy dungeon; two or three dolls lay by my side, along with a ball of rope and scissors. My tongue wetting my lips, my brow furrowed, I cut a piece of rope, one for each victim. I pushed myself to standing, my small dimpled hands pressing against the floor for support, then climbed on the chair I had placed beneath the pipes that ran exposed along the width and length of the ceiling. It was there that I hanged each doll in the basement gallows, absorbed in their dead, blank stares.

Where some of my play was designed to take control of my powerless, victim-centered experience, other times I used endorphin-releasing games to quiet my inner savage beast. I had a game I called TP, which stood for "taking pills." Like a homeless child rummaging for sustenance, my parents' medicine chest the dumpster, I would ingest. To understand my intent, never taking enough pills to die and knowing nothing about getting high, is to understand the bizarre thinking of an eight-year-old attempting to manage her anguish—the danger of the forbidden releasing a flow of soothing brain chemicals.

My parents' medicine chest was not the only way of quieting the chaos inside. I had become adept at relieving the neighborhood drugstore and gift shop of everything from candy to Christmas ornaments, toys to record albums, while never approaching the cash register, the big sleeves of my army fatigue jacket the perfect camouflage. Again, the rush of endorphins would flood my mind with a soothing calm. However, the relief never lasted long. With each successful attempt at anguish management came a stronger and more pronounced rebound of self-hatred and alienation. I knew I was different; I felt it on my skin.

I saw it in my reflection. At nine years old, even my front teeth aroused a sense of disgust. Scrutinizing them in the powder room mirror, my friend by my side, I made a decision. Leaving her wondering, I hurried to the basement, returning with hammer and screwdriver in hand. Our images casting back—mine with lips curved up and squinting eyes, hers with mouth gaping and eyes like saucers—metal to enamel, hammer in hand, I made contact.

My broken smile represented my inner experience—a life shattered by venomous emotions that were a constant threat to my sense of security. However, I had made an important discovery. Injury, I found, brought me a certain amount of pleasure, a release switch that allowed the pressure to burst out, if just for a moment. Too young still to understand that I could take those matters into my own hands, I offered it instead to the hands (and feet) of others. Knowing when peers were planning to beat up the weird girl, I would succumb to assaults that purged my body of my parasitic pain. If others weren't planning an assault on my soul, I helped them. Overnight camp, the summer between sixth and seventh grade, I taunted and teased one of the camp counselors to a point he could no longer withstand. As I made my way back to my cabin from a morning of swimming or sailing, the dirt path muffled the footsteps that had been following me. With a swift motion, strong hands from behind met me with a destabilizing force. I found myself curled up, fetal position, the taste of earth on my lips, as the fists and feet of the eighteen-year-old son of the Episcopalian minister who ran the camp swung savagely. I lay motionless, privately loving every minute as each violent contact expelled the evil that lay within.

With chaotic behaviors came chaotic relationships. My peers had to contend with my terrified ways of thinking and responding and the self-loathing that dripped from my pores. So elusive was the terror that stole my sensibility that I was forced to place it on more concrete matters—stray dogs, people, the outdoors, the indoors. I feared everything. Walking to

7

school alone or on an errand for the family caused a flare-up of internal activity that was most often met by a flare-up of external activity—pleading with friends to walk with me, raging at family for any request that left me unescorted—my needs, my behavior, too much to bear. The very thing I had feared with such intensity was indeed a daily reality. My only choice was to ignore the teasing and bullying, as I tolerated anything to avoid the rejection that came from everyone in my path—friends and family alike—my presence a toxic fume from which all living beings must flee. Abandonment had become more common than breathing, more terrifying than death.

By the middle of seventh grade, I got the news—I was to be plucked from the home I knew well. My family was moving. Despite all of its dark and desperate associations, I did not want to leave the security of the known. I begged and pleaded for us to stay where the anguish I experienced was familiar and predictable; the new harboring monsters I could not even imagine. Attempts at pleading my case landed squarely on deaf ears.

In my new school, I finally found an ally—Mr. Richardson, my eighth-grade history teacher. He seemed to take a liking to me, and I to him. I would sit in his classroom during free periods and talk to this man whose soft, drooping eyes reminded me of the sad look of a basset hound. For no other reason than the attention he paid me, I felt Mr. Richardson to be the only teacher—no, the only person—who understood me. The following year, once again the school placed me in Mr. Richardson's history class, having noticed the connection he was able to make, that he had somehow reached into the darkness and found me. However, there was a new history teacher. He was young and cute, and I wanted to be in *his* class, but my request was denied. Innocent though he was of any wrongdoing, I suddenly saw Mr. Richardson as an obstacle rather than an ally, and all the good I felt for him instantly split off from my mind. From that day on, I hated Mr. Richardson, the teacher who now had no idea who I was.

The skills I had acquired during my young life worked— from cigarettes to drugs, shoplifting to starvation, whatever I could do in the moment to manage the monster within, the unrelenting loneliness, the crippling fear of abandonment. Then, on a warm summer night, as I lay listlessly on the ground in a drunken stupor, broken glass scattered about, with little conscious awareness and no real plan of intent, I cut my flesh and watched the pain ooze out of the incision I had made. I realized in that moment how readily I could manage the mayhem that wreaked havoc in my mind, body, and soul. Exogenous chemicals, endogenous chemicals, whichever was going to provide the most immediate gratification.

Riddled with chaotic behaviors, I was screaming out for someone to notice the anguish with which I was struggling. It was not until the tenth grade, bloody-knuckled as I clung to sanity, arriving scabbed and scarred, that a meeting with my high school finally got my parents' attention: "Your daughter is exhibiting some very bizarre behaviors in school. She's cursing at the teachers in the middle of class, laughing at them, walking out in the middle of lessons, and has not handed in a single assignment since the beginning of the year. We can't keep her. We will, however, give you the chance to try and get her some help." This was the first time my parents allowed themselves to *see* their daughter. With the weight of an ultimatum resting on her shoulders and sufficient guilt to prod her along, my mother brought me to three different therapists, all of whom refused to treat me by the second or third visit—I was too angry, too out of control, *too sick* for treatment. On the brink of expulsion, with no hope and nowhere to turn— my anguish burning my core like a fire held firmly to the palm of one's hand—I overdosed on a bottle of sleeping pills in the lobby of my high school.

A bed now available on the adolescent unit, four men with keys dangling from their belts, and the air of authority dan-gling from their lips, offered me a choice: walk or we'll tie you up and carry you over. One of the men linked his fingers with mine, preventing escape, as I was led into the ranch-style building. It was then I found myself alone in a horror movie— incarcerated in a private psychiatric hospital.

Treatment became part of my disease. As I acted out, the staff played along, as we colluded in a dance of reenactments. It took little before I would find myself tethered to a bed in a seclusion room, paralyzed by leather restraints, somnolent due to chemical ones, or stripped bare in the name of safety, searching for injury, dousing me with shame. The immobiliza-tion and isolation mirrored the powerlessness and abandon-ment I experienced in my life. My identity became that of hospitalized mental patient. The times that I was well enough to be in the midst of society, I still found myself with the con-stant reminder that I was but an emotional invalid, unable to manage the most basic circumstances. My high school, a stark contrast to the private hospital where I was frequently incar-cerated, offered the clear message that others had little hope for my recovery.

The state hospital received its first patient on July 12, 1880. Walking along the grounds provides an unsettling aura of the asylum's disturbing past. One can hardly miss the ghosts of the thousands of mentally ill men and women who were "treated" with barbaric methods during its many years, from brutish times into the present. It was here, in one of the ominously beautiful buildings common to nineteenth-century asylum architecture, that I was made to attend high school. We were twelve of the most emotionally damaged children from my district, overseen by four specially trained teachers in two rooms in the basement of building 5. We were hardly assumed to survive our adolescence, much less to enter college. We were warehoused. And so it went, in and out, in and out, the degrading idiom "frequent flyer" not missed on me.

Then came the switch. I cannot say for sure how I got there or what the turning point was. Perhaps my mind, body, and soul could no longer take the assaults that were landing on me like flying fists, and my desperation for normality began to prevail. What I can say is the day came that, like a switch being flipped in my mind, appearing from what seemed to be a dark haze, I made a decision: *I do not want to be sick anymore.* This idea had been unavailable to me until the very moment it made itself known. Eventually I left the hospital, never to return. The road at that point, though, was far from smooth.

In my mind, recovery meant getting a job. I searched the Sunday classified ads with an internal barrage of bullets ricocheting in my gut. Slowly and methodically, so as not to self-destruct, I managed to attain employment at a family-run office supply store. With each day came the bubbling up of the all-too-familiar internal mayhem, restricting my calorie intake the only way to quiet it. Had anyone noticed, I might have been readmitted, as my weight slowly made its way down to that of a small child. But I was in recovery. Eventually, I became knowledgeable of the computerized cash register for which I was responsible, and food once again became part of my repertoire. As the year continued uneventfully, boredom replaced my notion of recovery. I left the office supply store.

My next chapter involved education. Though I had never taken the SATs or considered college, as my parents had been warned against this as a setup for disappointment, family connections made this next step to recovery a possibility. The same internal mayhem followed me from office supply store to university. My solution, however, had changed. Drugs. I would make my purchase on Thursday, using through Sunday, prepared for classes by Monday. Had anyone noticed, I might have been readmitted, as I had become a weekend junkie. But I was in recovery. Once I understood that college was possible, my grades proving my ability, I no longer needed my crutch, but rather a method of detox. I applied to the junior-year-abroad program, knowing that drugs would be less available to me in Europe. Within six years of this step in my recovery, and with just about as many majors, I finally graduated college with a degree in psychology—but you guessed that one, didn't you?

A job and college had given me enough confidence that I was able to present a normal side of myself to the man who approached me on a Thursday evening in April 1986, during a girls' night out. One year later, and the ring was on my finger. Two years later, and the wedding march was humming from the organ.

Now no longer diagnosable, I appeared a healthy young adult, hiding well my physical scars and my emotional ones too. My life had changed in dramatic ways. I found the love of my life, married him, and gave birth to three daughters. These were milestones I never thought I would live to see. Despite all that was well, my internal experience was something I privately still had to manage. As our girls grew older, I reentered therapy to finally process my childhood trauma that the behavioral methods of the 1970s and '80s had bypassed. Once my oldest became the age I was when first incarcerated, I became curious about the diagnosis I had been given thirty years prior, so I began to search—both for the meaning of borderline personality disorder and for as many people from my old treatment team as I could find, including my old psychiatrist, emerging like a ghost from the past. It was then that I knew my career path—I finally established myself as a mental health professional and as a guest lecturer offering a personal perspective on the treatment of trauma. Finally, still burdened with memories of institutionalization, I knew I had to rid my mind of the ruminative thoughts that would stir me from sleep. As my last step, and most cathartic venture, I put my experience on paper in my book, *The Boom Boom Retreat: A Memoir.*

At last, I have managed my anguish.

2. Letting the Light In

I was diagnosed with borderline personality disorder in 1990, when I was twenty-nine years old, following a suicide attempt. The overdose wasn't my first attempt at taking my life. Several years prior, I had tried to cut my wrists but was unable to go deep enough. I didn't tell anyone what I had done. Through that act, I discovered the ritual of cutting, which calmed the emotional ups and downs that were plaguing me as well as the emptiness that had invaded my soul.

I've been in different forms of psychotherapy since I was twenty-three, and after receiving the diagnosis of BPD, I wanted to know why. What had caused me to develop this illness that back then carried such a negative connotation in the psychiatric community? I wanted someone or something to blame. I wanted a reason to shove in a box, tie up with a pretty bow, and place high up on a shelf in the closet. I wanted the BPD out of sight and out of mind.

Life didn't work that way. A picture of a broken animal, its still body lying contorted by the side of the highway, came to mind as I endured repeated hospitalizations and frequent episodes of depression and anorexia. Chaos reigned. I wasn't actively suicidal, but when I went to bed each night, I begged to a power greater than myself not to wake up.

After my first two hospitalizations for anorexia, the loss of a promising career in marketing, and the suicide attempt, I went on the rolls of Social Security disability. I was a patient for almost a year on a long-term dialectical behavioral therapy hospital unit that specialized in treating BPD, until my insurance ran out, and then I lived in a halfway house for three and a half years. Part of the time I was staying in the residence, I was attending an outpatient DBT day program for people with BPD. In 1995, I left the residence and moved into my own apartment.

Three years later, while continuing with the intensive therapy I had started while on the long-term unit, I entered a graduate school program for social work. I was going to become a therapist. Being in therapy for so long had sparked a fascination with the process, and I wanted to help others as my therapists had helped me.

In 2000, I graduated with a perfect 4.0 GPA and found my first job at an outpatient mental health clinic near my home in Westchester, New York. They knew nothing of my history. My supervisor was a kind man, and I did well there until 2005, when the unrelenting depression returned and I needed to be hospitalized. I had known I felt off, but I didn't want to believe that my mental illness could interrupt my life again.

There was no doubt that I had to be admitted; there were suicidal thoughts involved. I hadn't been this depressed in a long time. My mother had passed away in 2002; perhaps it was a long-delayed reaction to her death. Or maybe it was just time for me to fall apart.

I returned to work after a month, but nothing had changed. Another hospitalization followed several months later, at the beginning of 2006. This time when I returned to work, I found that my clinical responsibilities had been severely curtailed. Humiliated, I resigned.

The internal chaos had assaulted my core once again. Without my job, which had defined me since my mother's death, I felt increasingly empty. This tidal wave of emotions brought the beginning of a complete breakdown, which required six hospitalizations in all and several years to return to my former level of functioning.

In 2007, when I was still on this roller coaster ride, I enrolled in a writing class at a local center. I enjoyed the feeling of creating something from nothing, of crafting a sentence, a paragraph, and a finished essay. I continued to take classes for two years and published several pieces. I didn't feel comfortable calling myself a writer, but I enjoyed the elation that came from seeing my name in print.

The writer identity began to snake its way into my psyche and slowly replaced the patient identity. I had found something else that I was good at and that was validated by others, by my instructor, by my classmates, and by seeing my work in the pages of an anthology.

I had started with a new therapist who was also a psychiatrist and a psychoanalyst. She specialized in transference focused psychotherapy, which is a psychodynamic treatment for BPD that focuses on the transference between the therapist and the client and the insights gained. The therapist highlights the behaviors that have become apparent in the therapeutic relationship and how they influence the client's relationships in her life outside the therapeutic office.

The therapy called for sessions twice a week. Dr. L encouraged me to free-associate, but that was difficult for me. I was used to censoring what I said, which went back to a fear of criticism from my father. He used to tell me to "Thimk," especially during our chess games, as my hand was poised over the board holding a rook or a pawn. He purposely mangled the word "think" so it stuck in my mind, and I rarely answered a question without hearing his harsh voice reverberating in my brain.

For many years, I used the "Thimk" excuse, which seemed plausible until Dr. L confronted me.

"I don't think you're thinking as much as you claim to be when I ask you a question," she said in a calm voice.

Disbelieving, I looked at her.

"It goes back to the chess games you played with your father, but more with your fear of angering him—and your fear of rejection from him—and from me."

Slowly, I nodded. "I was terrified of what he might say to me if I dared to say the wrong thing. I couldn't risk it. I couldn't risk that he might think I was stupid. If he thought I was stupid, he wouldn't love me. I wouldn't be his daughter anymore. He'd abandon me."

"Go on," Dr. L urged.

"Just like if I said the wrong thing to you, you'd reject me and abandon me."

"And you wouldn't be my daughter anymore?"

I burst into tears.

Dr. L encouraged me to return to my career as a social worker on a part-time basis at first. I found a fee-for-service job at an outpatient mental health clinic in Queens, not far from where I had grown up. It was a long drive from my home in Westchester, but they were willing to take a chance on me.

After nine months of working part-time, I was hired on a full-time basis. Soon after that, the executive director of the agency tapped me to start working on some administrative projects for her. She had noticed my penchant for perfectionism and my talent for detail-oriented work, and she put it to use. Slowly I stopped taking on clients and began taking on more administrative work. I enjoyed the feeling that I was contributing to the running of the clinic in a more global way. It felt as though I had finally found my niche.

Dr. L was pleased that I had come so far, but she had additional ideas about what fueled my tendency to enjoy this specific type of work.

"I think it makes you feel superior, just like the anorexia did," she told me.

"I admit that when I was in the midst of the anorexia, I got a kick out of feeling that I was better than other people because I could resist eating and because I could drop thirty pounds at will. But what does that have to do with this?" I asked.

"You're reviewing the work of other therapists. You're correcting their work and picking up on issues that they potentially overlooked."

"Yeah. So?" I was defensive.

"I think you get a kick out of that. You feel you know what you're doing while they know less than you do. It's a similar situation to when you were actively anorexic."

I crossed my arms over my chest and slumped down in my chair. "And what if I consider that you might be right?"

I learned that Dr. L was intelligent and rarely off the mark. A tall woman with short curly hair, she sat impeccably dressed in a comfortable black leather chair with her feet up on a matching ottoman. I sat facing her in a hard-backed, rather uncomfortable chair. At times I wondered if she purposefully chose that chair to keep her clients alert.

In the years I worked with Dr. L, my life began to ease into a predictable rhythm. I was doing well, functioning at a higher level than anyone would have thought possible. I was advancing at my job. I was writing and publishing. While not dating, I had a full and active social life with a small but close circle of friends and family. And I was able to reduce my sessions with Dr. L to once a week.

We talked about my lack of interest or desire to date. "You know," she said to me during one session, "you deny yourself two of the greatest pleasures of life: food and sex. What is that about?"

"I'm afraid," I replied. "Of becoming dependent on a man, of making myself vulnerable to him. I don't think I'm capable of an intimate relationship." I paused. "I'm afraid of consuming him and of him consuming me."

"That sounds an awful lot like food," Dr. L remarked.

In 2012, my father was starting to make noise from his apartment in Queens. His health was declining, and he needed my brother's and my assistance. My work was close by, so several nights a week I did his food shopping for him. His apartment was in a state of squalor. I couldn't believe that I had grown up there, playing on my hands and knees on the white tile floors that were now black with grime and littered with dead roaches.

My brother convinced our father to move up to a studio apartment in Connecticut, closer to him. Dad's health declined quickly up there, and one afternoon in 2013, I took him to the hospital. He never left. He had sepsis, and his liver was failing. Transferred to a palliative care facility, he died within ten days. My brother and I tossed his ashes in the Long Island Sound on a brisk spring afternoon.

The depression took root six months after my father's death, as snow and ice covered the ground and life died from the bitter chill. I had been well for so long, I believed that I was safe. Day after day at work, I shut the door to my office and sobbed. Dr. L admitted me to a partial hospitalization program. She changed my medication.

I returned to work for a week and felt overwhelmed. Before the sun rose on a Saturday morning, I padded into my kitchen and swallowed a bottle of pills. Wading back into my bedroom, I fell down onto my bed and waited to die. I took a cab to the emergency room and wound up on the cardiac floor attached to a heart monitor. I was transferred to a psychiatric hospital. Dr. L had mandated that I be admitted to the personality disorders unit.

My BPD symptoms, the ones I thought I was managing so well, had erupted in a torrent as though an aorta had torn with blood everywhere. I had fired Dr. L several months back in a burst of anger, and although we had seemingly worked it out, I hadn't realized how very angry I still was with her. The internal emptiness, the pain—the night prior to the overdose, I had lain on my living room floor, hand outstretched toward my cat, howling as though I were a wounded animal, my snot dripping into the carpet.

For the first time in the nine-plus years that I had been working with Dr. L, I began to talk about my anger. Toward her, toward the people I loved, toward the world in general. She didn't judge me, reject me, or abandon me. I told her I was a terrible person, hateful, and I should be condemned for having such thoughts. She didn't laugh or even smile. She took me seriously, and I felt validated.

I hadn't written since December of 2013, and I was mourning the loss of my creativity. I was mourning the loss of the identity that had once rescued me from being a patient. Now I was ill once again, and my only way out was to talk about it.

I worked hard at saying the first thought that came to mind. Without censoring. Without judging myself. Sessions passed. Weeks. Months. I asked my boss if I could return to work full-time in August. Prior to that, I had been at my job only part-time. Feeling inspired once more, I began to post my blog weekly. It felt freeing to be writing again.

I visualized the morning mist rising off the ocean, curling up to meet the clouds. My black-and-white thinking faded to gray. I was able to envision both sides of a concept more easily, to see a compromise where before there had been only absolutes. I realized how deeply my father must have been hurt when the psychiatrist on the long-term BPD unit accused him of sexually abusing me as a child. I realized that his fragile ego most likely never recovered, and in response, he chose to retreat. "Daddy, I'm sorry." Too late. He could no longer hear me. The hatred I once felt for him was dwarfed by my shame.

I recently turned fifty-four, and my core sentiment is one of gratitude. I look back over the last twenty-five years, and I am thankful for all the people in my life who stayed with me when I was determined to destroy myself. I thought I was thriving when I was treading water. I thought there could be no more surprises when there were countless bombshells waiting to be unearthed.

Dr. L commented that this last year has been the most intense. I've done a great deal of work. I still have work to do. I will always have work to do. To preserve equilibrium, to maintain balance, to let the light in. What is different now is I like the person I have become. I respect her. When I recall the level of pain the woman on the carpet was in a year ago, the memory brings tears to my eyes. I am content now, and I pray every day that I will never be face down on that carpet again.

3. I Am Not Just a Box in the DSM-5

I thought they were mistaken when the doctors first began tossing around the term "borderline personality disorder" in reference to me. I didn't—couldn't—have that. That was what Winona Ryder, playing Susanna Kaysen, in *Girl, Interrupted* had. I may be crazy, but I never chased a bottle of aspirin with a bottle of vodka, dismissing this act by famously proclaiming, "I had a headache."

Let me clarify: it is not that I wouldn't do or say this, or that I haven't pulled equally as lethal and inexplicable stunts to eradicate my suffering; I just had never thought to combine these two.

It didn't help that initially the case manager threw around the diagnosis in the manner he would if he were trying to decide whether a yellow or blue scarf would set off my eyes more. His insensitivity aside, it felt like he was criticizing my life—both past and future—into a confused paralysis between neurotic and psychotic. You may raise your eyebrows at this dramatic description. I challenge you to Google how the term "borderline" was originally coined and then come talk to me about the implications of being placed into this category.[1]

As I set out on my twelfth path through structured treatment, I struggled with what it meant to be borderline. No amount of self-discovery, excruciating examination of my thoughts, behaviors, or emotional experience seemed to shed much light on what this *DSM* box meant.[2] The trouble with semantics in psychiatry is that we often take no notice of how minor parts of speech or turns of phrase change the definition of what it means to live these diagnoses on a daily basis. That is, however, until those things become what feels like the defining part of who you are. When someone is diagnosed with depression, you won't hear them say, "I am depression." This is equally unlikely with a patient diagnosed with anorexia or bipolar disorder or even schizophrenia. A rare few psychiatric conditions enjoy the pleasure of being both an adjective describing one's mood or classification of behaviors and a noun—a label—to encompass all of who one is. Alcoholics. Addicts. And borderlines. Unfortunately for me, I identify with all of these conditions.

But even as I write this, I find myself battling my own definition of being borderline. I have never allowed myself to fall neatly into a box of any type—or, more accurately, have never wanted to. For example, I am blond, but I would more likely slap someone than allow them to stereotype me as a Barbie manifestation or a dumb blonde. Same with the stereotypes attached to being classified as Boston Irish Catholic (if I had a nickel for the number of times I have been asked why I don't have a Boston accent, I would be a very rich woman). The trouble is that much of my behavior is so "classically borderline" that it's tough to break away from this label. Desperate attempts to avoid abandonment? Check. Untrusting? Dramatic? Reactive? Check, check, check. Unrelenting standards for self and others that cause massive vacillations between idealization and devaluation? Triple check. So I find myself questioning whether and how I can be more than my diagnosis.

I don't have the perfect self-proclamation to tie this story into a neat little bow. I am more than borderline, just like I am more than my hair, eye, or skin color, or where I went to school and who my parents are. I think my therapists, psychiatrists, or pretty much anyone who has ever met me will tell you that. Despite this, it is still a daily struggle to see myself beyond "borderline." Nor do I seek to oversimplify or dismiss the anguish of my experience or that of others. Most days, I don't see this silver lining. But I have to hold on to the hope that I am and will be more to myself, to my family, and to the world than just a diagnosis or a McLean Hospital patient. I've never settled for a box before, and I am certainly not about to start now.

The strategies I need to create a better life for myself have always been readily available. I just didn't know how or when to access them. Going through treatment helped me develop a toolkit of coping mechanisms that were healthy and not destructive. Who knew that something besides drowning my emotions in alcohol could work? For so many years, my instinct was to drown any and all intense emotions in substances or to starve them away. Makes a lot of sense, right? To someone deep in the throwes of my disease, it did. But now I know that drinking my problems away just makes them worse. Because eventually I have to come out of the fog, out of the blackout. And when I do, I feel all of the things that I set out to escape—sadness, emptiness, toxic shame, anger—plus an added round of guilt and humiliation for having drunk at all.

So what is my alternative? Today I can call my friend Anne, whom I met at a treatment facility. Anne actually knows me. The me beneath all the layers of the onion, the layers of the badass preppy girl. She has been in group with me when I am insatiably chatty about psychological stuff, because I have to know everything—and she still likes me. Anne and I share the misfortune of both being from snobby Boston suburbs, though she wears it with ironic appreciation as opposed to my disdain. She has an energy about her that makes it impossible not to like her. She is engaging and interesting when she wants to be. And if I hadn't gone through the Gunderson program, I would never have met her or any of the other fantastic people I met there. So the people I have met in treatment are my silver lining, because without them, I would not be who I am today.

I oftentimes wonder what would have or could have happened if I had "taken" to treatment during my first go-round. Or my fifth. Or even my ninth. Would I be on *Forbes*' top 30 under 30 for politics? Would I have realized sooner that I wanted to work with people directly, helping them improve their own circumstances? Would my former romantic and platonic relationships have fallen apart in the dramatic ways that they did, or would I be married and be on my way to having the family that I so desperately crave? Maybe. But this exercise is futile; it is more an exercise in self-flagellation than a constructive use of my time. My road through hell and back happened the way that I needed it to. I needed to reach all of those Inferno-like bottoms to truly realize that I could not and did not want to continue living the way that I was. If I had been asked three years ago what I was willing to do to recover from my diseases, I might have been willing to stop drinking. Or stop starving myself. Or even stop using romantic interactions to try to fill the bottomless hole in my heart. But I was not ready to fundamentally rebuild my interpersonal interactions or to change my coping skills, and, most importantly, I was not willing, ready, or able to experience my emotions. I was still trapped in my emotionless fantasy world, where I could shut pain and suffering off, like a light switch. In DBT therapy, we are taught that emotions are like waves and can be ridden. So my emotional pain should ebb and flow, like the tides?

The DBT gurus from the Gunderson Residence at McLean Hospital teach patients how to ride these emotional waves without making things worse. This is a noble lesson, and likely incredibly useful for 95 percent of the borderline patients who go through an intensive DBT program. But for me, it took more than didactic lessons to learn to implement this into my life. I had to make mistakes and learn from them in real time—oftentimes to the horror of my treatment team and family. Oftentimes, these mistakes, my failures to adhere to the treatment protocol, baffled my treatment team and parents. I believe—though I do not know—that all these people occasionally blamed themselves for my self-destructive behavior. I probably blamed them too at times. I resented them calling me "one of the most complicated cases in their thirty years of experience." As I look back now, it was not their fault. Mostly, I was hell-bent on protecting my own misery, because it was the only dependable companion I have ever known. Even if I think back to my "happy" high school years, that self-critical, self-loathing voice was my closest companion.

Driving a wedge between my true self and this negative, hate-fueled version of myself was a truly Herculean effort. It took years to put enough space between the two selves for me to even begin to recognize the existence of this voice. It took months of true ambivalence about life to wake up one morning and look at myself in the mirror and see the utter defeat and sadness that had taken over. It took another round of treatment in an alcohol facility to grasp some wisp of hope that if I could cut the shit, stop the self-destruction, I could have a better life. My true self deserves better. The little girl who danced around effortlessly in pink and purple sparkles deserves better. The girl who talked to strangers, just because, deserves better. The person who dreamed of changing the world through hard work and devotion to equality deserves better.

At one treatment center I went to, the psychiatrist, after hearing my story in its entirety, asked me, point-blank, how I was possibly still breathing. I shrugged and said, "I don't know." This may seem cavalier; I am a lot of things, but cavalier is not one of them. I honestly don't know how I survived all the physical torture I put my body through. I don't know that I believe in a "higher power." I don't believe in fate. Much to my mother's chagrin, I know organized religion is not my thing. But there has to be some greater purpose to my life than what it has been so far. And in the darkest of my days—of which there have been many—I have always found solace in the small ways of making life better for other people. So if my story, if my pain, can help save someone else from making the same mistakes that I have, then I guess it was worth it.

Today, I woke up energetic. Today, I did not plot how I could become invisible. I can once again look people in the eye. Don't get me wrong—I still have my moments of despair. Sometimes I still put my headphones in on the Metro ride without actually playing music so that no one will talk to me. I do not look in the mirror in the morning chanting loving mantras at myself. But I can look in the mirror without seeing the sum of all my flaws. I can look in the mirror and see beyond all the psychiatric and other sorts of labels that people have ascribed to me. Yes, I may be a borderline, raging alcoholic, depressive, former anorexic patient. But I am also a friend. A daughter. A sister. A niece. A cousin. A soon-to-be teacher. A lifelong student. I am becoming dependable. I am ambitious. I am intelligent. I am a woman.

My life and path to recovery has followed a dark, twisted road. But each wrong turn has made me stronger. At the end of the day, I am who I am today because of what I have lived through. Someday, I will be able to look at it all and be grateful. Someday, I will look in that mirror and be proud of what I have been through. When that day comes, I may just surprise myself and be happy to be me, in spite of any box the world tries to put me in. Until then, I am okay with who I am. I will never be able to live up to my narcissistic ideal of who I should be. But I would rather be me than anyone else. That is the true accomplishment of all the treatment I have gone through. For that, all my treaters over the years should be proud. Because I am proud.

4. You Talk and Don't Know That I Listen

I recently read an article about a girl with multiple sclerosis who runs races and collapses in pain at the end of every race. My every day is a race and at the end of every day, I collapse on my bed, in so much agony, and I never want to get through any other day. But I do. I have to. That's what living with borderline personality disorder feels like. It feels like an endless fight. It feels like I've been treading in stormy waters for days, and I am getting so tired, but no one is around to throw me a life raft, because no one wants to be around me. This runner with MS has a coach who catches her after every race. My only net is the emptiness of my bed and the hollowness of my pillow. Although this runner and I share a similar experience, my story and my experience would never be reported on for public display.

I was diagnosed in my senior year of college, after a bit of a suicide attempt. My therapist was talking about reducing our sessions, and I believed she didn't want to see me anymore, that she was abandoning me. That's one of the biggest symptoms of BPD. So I went home, brokenhearted. Then the following day, my mom snapped at me for something I didn't do, and that pushed me over the edge. I was brought to the hospital by ambulance, treated terribly in the acute psychiatric wing, and then sent along to a mental health inpatient facility where the diagnosis was handed to me. I still remember the psychiatrist sitting in front of me asking, "Have you ever heard of borderline personality disorder?" Yes, I had, and I got so mad at her. The term had been thrown around in front of me a few times in high school. But that was in response to my self-injurious behaviors, another symptom of BPD. I told her she was wrong and that she was just pushing my buttons. I stormed out of her office. However, after thinking it through and really looking at how I had gotten to where I was, I realized that she was right. I went back to her and calmly sat down as we talked more about it.

Now, you would think that hearing the diagnosis of borderline personality disorder would have broken me more. After all, hearing it initially made me angry and defensive. That was a diagnosis you really didn't want to have. But once I calmed down, I was relieved in a way. I had an answer. I had something tangible that described everything I felt, everything I did, and every way I acted. I thought to myself, "Wow, I'm not crazy—it's just this disorder." I was actually almost proud of my diagnosis, because now I had something to fight for. I knew what to attack this time and what to work on. So, I went to work. I was discharged from the hospital and spent the next twelve weeks at an intensive outpatient program where dialectical behavior therapy was infused in my brain. I also wasn't allowed to come back to school unless I obliged. I had already had some exposure to DBT, but this was even more enlightening. I learned so much, and I had so much more control over my borderline. My IOP stood by me until I graduated. The staff at my IOP inspired me to follow in their footsteps. While in the program, I decided to apply to the graduate school of social work. I wanted to be like those who had treated me, and now that I knew what the experience was like as the client, I could do the same thing for someone like me.

I was ecstatic when I received the acceptance letter, and I quickly enrolled and got to work. There were some providers of mine who didn't think it was the best idea, but I didn't care. This is what I wanted to do. It was interesting sitting in class hearing about human behavior and social policies. It was great being at an internship where I could work with kids and help them through different interpersonal altercations with friends. Those DBT interpersonal-effectiveness skills came in real handy. It wasn't until I got to my first social work practice class that I hit a huge brick wall and was slapped with reality. My teacher was talking about how there are certain clients that you just can't handle. He elaborated by saying that no one can work with everyone, and he felt he couldn't work with—you guessed it—clients with borderline personality disorder. He talked about how manipulative they were and how exhausting they were. He told us that if we were to have any borderlines at all that we should take only one because that's all we would be able to handle. He talked about borderlines as though they were malicious creatures sucking the life out of everyone around them. So that's what I felt like, sitting in the middle of his class, like a ton of bricks, like a rug had been pulled out from under me. Is that what borderlines are really like? Is that what I'm like? I tried to work these thoughts and feelings out with my therapist, but the insults would not stop there.

After that, I heard teachers talk about how manipulative borderline clients were and how you had to think really hard before saying anything to them. Then I heard a field instructor of mine say that she couldn't stand working with borderlines, because they just exhausted her. Then one student's comment in class completely broke me. She said that she needed to take a whole bottle of Xanax before working with a client with borderline personality disorder. My mouth had dropped to the floor, and a knife had been plunged through my heart. Did people feel that way about me? Could I not stop myself from turning into this beast everyone was talking about?

Instead of letting these thoughts, words, judgments, and hatred defeat me, I decided they would fuel me to fight for those suffering from borderline personality disorder, to fight for me. I started telling people that if they felt a borderline was overwhelming and exhausting, then they weren't the right people to work with them, because they weren't qualified. I brought information about dialectical behavior therapy and its positive impact on those suffering with BPD to every class, every paper, every discussion, every assignment, and every conversation. Well, maybe not every conversation... There goes my borderline brain, being overly dramatic and thinking only on the two extremes, right! But I did try to fight every comment and every judgment. It was an extra part-time job, a few more hours of work to do per week, on top of a full-time course load, part-time internships, and two part-time jobs. That fight took a big toll on me, not so much on my work ethic or dedication to the cause, but it stripped me of my confidence and pride in having the disorder. I questioned every move I made and analyzed every comment that came out of my mouth. I didn't want anyone to know that I was one of those dreaded borderlines. I was walking on eggshells, everywhere, making sure my secret was safe with me. It was really hard, and it made me really depressed. Why did people have to feel this way? Why did future social workers have to feel this way? Why were they learning about the difficulty of borderlines? Why were they being taught to stay away from borderlines? Why were they taught to hate them, to hate me?

I still struggle and evaluate every remark I make, but I have gained some of my fight back. I have even disclosed to my closest friend at school. After a year and a half of getting to know her, I finally trusted her enough with that secret. Her reaction lifted me up so that I regained all of my strength. She told me that she was even more proud of me for my accomplishments, because she couldn't even imagine how hard it might be to work so hard at school while working so hard on your own personality. I am so thankful for this friend and so thankful for the honest reaction she had. I eventually also disclosed to a teacher at the end of a semester, and she reacted the same way. She said that I had a lot to be proud of if I had already achieved so much and conquered such a difficult and judged disorder. I am thankful to her as well. It is because of these two ladies and the incredible work I've done with my therapist that I've gotten to where I am today. I haven't fully recovered, and it is a continued uphill battle, but one that I can take in stride.

So, I have a dream I would love to share with you. I have worked very hard at school, created many relationships, and gone above and beyond to get involved. I would say that my name is known throughout the school. For that reason, my dream is to be chosen as the student speaker at our graduation ceremony, and in that dream I would say the following:

My fellow friends, classmates, peers, and acquaintances, we have finally made it to this moment. We have worked hard, slept little, stressed over how many articles we've had to read for every single class, and sweated over LSW test preparations. And now here we are, ready to go out into the real world to work, to heal, to help, and to serve. I have been on one hell of a ride with all of you, gone through sharp turns, backflips, downfalls, side twists, and more, and now here I am in front of you, honored for the opportunity to speak with you. I have learned a lot about all of you, about our professors, about the world, and, believe it or not, about me. I have received words of wisdom, words of truth, and words from the soul. They may not have always been the best words, but they needed to be heard. I'm here to tell you that they were heard, and they were inscribed into my heart and soul.

Those magnificent words felt like a fist flying across my cheek. Those words brought me further down and down so that I could feel the dirt pooling in my socks. Do you know what words I am talking about? No, of course not. Why would you? It's because you didn't know your words applied to me. It's because you didn't realize how loudly you spoke those words. It's because you didn't think those words had consequences. Are you ready to know what those words are? Those words were about a diagnosis that I have, a diagnosis that has been hard to control and hard to manage. I was diagnosed with borderline personality disorder in 2013, which isn't very long ago. And I have to say, at first I was relieved to have the diagnosis. I finally knew why I was experiencing all of these symptoms and thoughts. You all took that relief away from me with your words. You all made me doubt every thought, every action, every comment I made. It was brutal and exhausting, having to walk around with that secret. But at this moment, I feel powerful. I bet that none of you knew this about me, except one good friend whom I disclosed to. Do you feel bad that you said those words now? Do you wish you had said something different?

As I said, those words were hard to hear. But I have to say thank you to you all for those words, as well, because they made me stronger and more confident. Those words solidified my purpose in being a social worker. I and my words are a lesson to you. I have no doubt that with the knowledge we received here, we will be great social workers. But be careful. Watch your words, think before you speak, and think before you act. You never know who might be around you.

Here have been my words to you, and I hope they have found you well. Let my words give you strength, give you hope, give you faith. Let my words guide you to learn and to grow, as your words did for me. It's the least I can do. Onward and upward, let's step through the door and keep what we learned here close, because that knowledge will go a long way.

5. Dangerous to Delightful

Childhood Years

My memory of my early years is patchy. I am told that I was an emotionally sensitive child who was often tearful. I was often alone at school playtime and have a vivid island of memory of sitting alone crying for no apparent reason. The school contacted my parents about my crying and distress. The "wisdom" of the adults was that I was "attention-seeking"—the answer that was given to my distress so many times over the next twenty-five years.

Despite doing well academically, I had few friends and constantly felt inferior. I believed I was ugly and boring and felt privileged if someone even spoke to me. I was quiet and moody; I was now also becoming substantially obese. I hated my body, myself, and all aspects of my life.

Adult Years

My family saw me as dangerous, in that problems would arise for them if they had contact with me, which was true. They ceased all contact with me, and I was not invited to or even informed of my brother's and sister's weddings. I heard at a party that I had become an Aunty and was devastated that I was not able to see my niece. I had few friends and was unable to contribute to meaningful relationships or friendships. Some of my oldest friends continued to have limited contact, and I spent many nights crying over my inability to have any significant friendships. Many of my friends were in significant relationships, and I so dearly wished that I were capable of loving and being loved. I felt worthless.

As I had always done well academically, I awaited my final year results, expecting to pass and then to proceed through the formality of graduation. When the results came out, I got a dreadful shock. Whilst I had passed my exams, the nursing school declared that I was not a "fit and responsible" person, so I had not been granted a practicing certificate. The thin veneer of coping fell rapidly away in the face of this news, confirming my inner belief that I was worthless. And that the nursing school had formally declared me to not be a fit and responsible person confirmed growing beliefs that I was not only worthless but something worse—dangerous. The world needed protecting from me. My family, schoolteachers, and now the nursing profession had responded to me in a manner indicating that they saw me as dangerous. They needed to protect themselves from me. This pattern was to continue in later years with mental health professionals.

By this time, I had been admitted several times to a psychiatric ward. I settled into ward life and felt accepted by the other patients on the ward. The hospital became a safe place where I was cared for and looked after. I had over fifty admissions to the hospital in a ten-year period.

Over the next few years, I became really dependent on the inpatient unit, with the staff being the only family I now had. The hospital became a place that was too safe, where I took no responsibility for myself and had no need to take control of my life. This fed my belief that I was inadequate and unable to cope with life. The more my needs were met in the hospital, the less I believed I could manage my own life. This led to an increased frequency and duration of admissions, leading me to believe I was getting sicker, thereby needing more help, et cetera, et cetera—a never-ending cycle of helplessness and hopelessness—which heightened my risk of suicide.

I had many years where I felt unable to get out of bed, let alone contribute in any meaningful way to society. I felt that I was a failure, as I was receiving a benefit, and felt I was bludging off society. My life was an existence about which I was ashamed.

I now had different treatment expectations, which focused more on community treatment and supporting me to learn skills and be responsible for myself. Importantly, after many years in the mental health system, I was given a diagnosis of borderline personality disorder.

Part of me was horrified. In my nursing training, I had been taught that people with borderline personality disorder were difficult to be around, never got better since treatment was ineffective, and consequently were to be avoided—a wastebasket diagnosis. I had shifted from being a basket case to a wastebasket case—sounds funny now, but it wasn't at the time. However, a small part of me was incredibly grateful that I now had a name for the lifelong pain I had endured. This proved to be a turning point in my recovery.

Hope: A Treatment Plan and Self-Responsibility

On entering the hospital for the umpteenth time, the newly arrived psychiatrist encouraged and supported me to use psychological solutions more than medication solutions. I no longer expected a magical medication cure.

The next major turning point in my treatment was when my treating team decided that they had to stop readmitting me to the hospital so frequently and for so long. I thank them for their courage to take this step. They decided to develop a treatment plan that made it clear that if I initiated it in an appropriately assertive way, and had clear goals of how it would help, I could choose to have a voluntary admission to the hospital for a brief time-limited period. So I stepped into a new world—that of treatment plans and risk shared by the clinical teams and myself.

Within a few days of my discharge from the hospital with this plan that was designed, in my mind, to withhold support from me, I suffered a personal tragedy. A friend of mine died unexpectedly. In desperation and with mounting panic, I rang the crisis team. I had never dealt with minor difficulties using my own resources, and now I was outside the hospital and dealing alone (or so I felt) with this tragedy.

How quickly the wheels sprang into motion. A meeting of the team, including me (me—yes, me—I was a part of the team!) was organized for that afternoon, and increased levels of support were to be provided in the form of visits from the crisis team and a respite nurse to be with me at a respite facility (a place to go for some "time out" and support in a more normal and less restrictive environment than the hospital).

For the first time, I started to come on board, so to speak. These people, who, I had been convinced, were going to abandon me at the first opportunity, were actually trying to help and ensuring also that I had a major role in decision-making. I did utilize the extra support that was offered and did choose to spend a few days in the hospital over the time of the funeral. Seeds of trust with the community team were sown.

In the year following the development of my treatment plan, I used four brief admissions to the hospital. All of them were instigated by me before a crisis and had specific goals set by me, and for all of them, I was discharged on the day I had suggested before my admission, with the goals having been met.

Small successes served to encourage and motivate me to more successes. The longer I did not self-harm, the more determined I became.

At around the same time, I had begun working part-time. I began to form some friendships. I now had a vision of a future, something I did not have before, and started making some long-term goals.

Success bred success, and having spent so many years on a downward spiral, where hopelessness bred more hopelessness, I was now on my way up.

Repairing My Relationship with My Mother

You will recall that I had been estranged (not speaking) from my family for many years, and as I began to heal, this was a source of great anguish to me. I shed many tears over the damage I had done to those relationships. Eighteen months after the treatment plan had been put in place, I was engaged in a very tearful telephone conversation with my mother. She had cancer and was terminally ill. Surprisingly to me, in view of our estrangement, she desperately wanted to see me. We had a tearful face-to-face reunion the next day.

She wanted me to nurse her through her final months. What a two-edged sword. I was being given a wonderful gift, but the "gift" included my mother dying. Here was a dream come true, to be reunited with my family, but my mother was dying.

I met my brother's wife, my sister's husband, and my two-year-old niece, all for the first time. Despite my absence, life had gone on, and despite all the healing that has subsequently occurred, it saddens me to this day that I missed the weddings of my brother and sister and the first two years of my darling niece's life.

I was fortunate to spend around four somewhat contented months enjoying being part of my family, with things as normal as they can be when the matriarch's impending death hangs over you. Once my mother needed intense nursing, I was glad that I had refreshed some of my skills and regained some confidence in my ability as a skilled nurse. We celebrated my birthday as a family—something that was very special to me, as I had not had contact with my family on my birthday for sixteen years.

I continued to have regular contact with the two clinicians who had supported me so much. Whilst it had been some time since I had anything that could be considered a crisis, their continuity and stableness in my life was important to me.

By now, I had not self-harmed for almost two years. Mum and I spent many hours talking, and as her days drew to a close, I felt comfortable in the knowledge that she loved me as much as my brother and sister. I felt a wound healing—my relationship with my mother was repaired. Definitely late, but definitely not too late.

No doubt, the time pressure brought about by her impending death clearly led my mother to think about reconciliation and repair; however, without my substantial recovery, I am quite sure this would not have been able to happen. I finally had a place where I felt valued in my family. My mother depended on and wanted me for her physical cares, and the rest of the family needed me around to feel Mum was getting the best care. Can you believe it? My family, who would have nothing to do with me over all those years, now saw me as the most suitable person to give her the best possible care. These tragic circumstances further imbedded my sense of value as a person.

I end the story of my recovery years on a bittersweet note. The very thing I had desired all my adult life—a family—I now had and was an integral part of. However, the mother I had so recently made peace with—finding some peace within myself in doing so—was fading fast. On the tenth of November 1999, in the early hours of the morning, my mother died in my arms.

Epilogue

In the fifteen years since, things have continued to get better, day by day and step by step, and the skills that assisted in my recovery remain very much part of my toolbox.

Two of the aspects of living a life defined by the traits of borderline personality disorder that had been the most devastating for me were my inability to have meaningful relationships and my inability to contribute to society, primarily by having paid employment.

I have now been working full-time for most of the last fifteen years. The most troubling aspects of my life now are not that I find it difficult to get out of bed but rather about ensuring that I maintain a work-life balance. I have moved from management to nationwide health service monitoring roles. As a nurse I have "made it" to heights that most nurses aspire to. To this day, I feel privileged to be able to work and contribute to society. On the odd day when I feel a little (as most people do from time to time) overwhelmed by my workload, I can quickly reenergize myself by reflecting for a moment or two on how far I have come to be able to have a job I love and that is respectfully remunerated. I have also continued studying and have gained postgraduate qualifications relevant to my area of work and to health management. I have discovered that I love learning and that being mentally stimulated by a demanding job and concurrent study provides a sense of well-being that I never dreamed possible.

I continue to have a close relationship with my family. Recently, I mentioned to a colleague that I had spent many years estranged from my family, and she was amazed—having seen me interact occasionally with family members, she presumed that we had always been a closer family than most. I continue to play a large part in the lives of my sister's two children, and when issues arise, it is frequently the "problem solver" in the family (that is me) that other members of the family will turn to for clarity and solutions. I am delighted to also have been in a loving and healthy romantic relationship for the last eight years. Many years of healing allowed me to value myself and to be able to both give and accept love from my amazing partner. To have someone describe me as delightful almost defies belief.

Life has not been without struggles, but as my health has developed, I am able to meet the challenges head-on with a knowledge that I am a valued member of society who family, friends, employers, and colleagues believe is able to cope with life's hurdles and provide support to those I come in contact with. My journey continues…

6. Persisting Hope

From my journal in April 1999:

Somewhere along the way, I must have deemed myself worthy of happiness, because here I am in the center of emotional reincarnation. I'm changing. And I'm terrified of it. I am losing touch with the world I have known. I am being challenged to look beyond my illness, and I am scared of what I will find. Am I looking toward love, happiness, and stability? Do I even know what that means? I am stepping out of darkness into the light, and it's blinding. That is where I am now. Sleeves rolled up, immersed in the work of my soul. The pain I spent a lifetime building up must now be dissected in a matter of months. It is the demolition of my emotional walls and the destruction of what I have known as safety. I am tortured by my thoughts and plagued by my feelings. And my escape routes have been disposed of. This process is known as getting better. I am rebuilding the life I never knew.

I wrote those words while I was attending an intensive DBT day-treatment program. I was eighteen years old, struggling with a myriad of extreme emotional states and difficult behaviors, and not at all sure that there was life beyond it. I am now thirty-four years old, and I can tell you without a shadow of a doubt that there is.

I was diagnosed with borderline personality disorder at the age of sixteen. It was during my first inpatient hospitalization, and I was thrilled by it (both the hospitalization and the diagnosis). When I got out, I went to my local bookstore and pulled out a copy of the *DSM*. I vividly remember flipping through the pages and finding the diagnostic criteria for borderline personality disorder. Frankly, it was one of the best moments of my life. Here I was, in these pages! *Frantic efforts to avoid real or imagined abandonment.* Check. *Unstable and intense interpersonal relationships.* Check. *Impulsivity, anger, self-mutilation, unstable self-image, chronic feelings of emptiness.* Yes. This was me. It was a huge relief. I was borderline.

I had felt alone and isolated by my experiences for as long as I could remember. From the age of eight, when I had my first clear suicide plan, after getting kicked out of boarding school due to my "emotional problems" and ending up in the hospital, I knew there was something wrong with me and I had no idea how to fix it. But if I was in this book that so clearly and clinically stated my difficulties, it meant there were other people like me. And if there were other people like me, there were probably people who knew how to fix me.

There was nothing I wanted more than to be fixed. I have a memory of being on the school bus in high school, leaning my head against the window and fantasizing about having a lobotomy. I was so hopeful that someone could remove the "bad" parts of my brain and leave the rest. I was desperate to stop having such big feelings, to stop being so obsessive, to stop crying and yelling and driving people away. I was tired of hearing that I was "too much" for everyone. I was tired of being me.

Fast-forward a few years. In seeking help, treatment, deliverance, escape, I managed to get quite a few mental-patient milestones under my belt. After an involuntary stay in a state psychiatric hospital, my sixth suicide attempt, electroconvulsive therapy, and more self-inflicted injuries than I could count, I found my way to DBT.

I don't have a ton of memories from this period of my life. The addition of heavy psych meds may have something to do with that. But when I look over the homework that I saved from those days, some things jump out at me. My life skills were limited, and it was a brutal process to create them. I did worksheets on things as simple as how to bum a cigarette from someone and not freak out if they said no. I had to learn that I deserved to have my needs met and simultaneously get used to the idea that, even if I acted as skillfully as possible, they still might not be met. All of it was extremely difficult and painful. Beyond that, I was also being challenged to step away from my main coping mechanisms, namely cutting and burning myself.

I loved self-injury, and I was incredibly proud of my scars and my war stories. I would tell anyone who would listen about the time I burned the word "evil" into my arm so as to warn everyone about what I was. But that scar wasn't there anymore, and most of the others were fading. I always put aloe and vitamin E on my cuts as they healed. There was a part of me that knew that, although I loved showing off my scars now, there might be a time in my life when I wouldn't want them.

Now, let me be clear. At the time, the clinicians in that program would probably not have called me a success story. I was, more or less, kicked out of the program for shoplifting, smoking pot, and hiding alcohol all over my halfway house. I was still a mess, and the struggle was far from over. Post-DBT, I had one suicide attempt, a number of hospitalizations, and still quite a bit of upheaval. Getting sober helped, and so did more therapy.

Throughout my early twenties, the focus shifted away from the ways I was crazy and onto the ways I wasn't. My therapist would say over and over that even my internal life wasn't as weird as I thought it was. My eyes were opening to how fluid labels can be and the possibility that maybe "mental patient" was no longer a good fit for me.

In 2006, I decided to try going off my meds, under doctors' supervision. It ended up being something of a failed experiment, and in early 2007, I ended up in the hospital. A big part of me felt like a failure. It had been at least five years since my last inpatient stay, and I had thought that that part of my life was over. But I remember saying something that shows how much had changed. I said, "I'm not going to the hospital because I'm afraid I'll kill myself. I'm going to the hospital because I'm afraid I'll wreck the beautiful life I've built." I was starting to have a life worth living, and I was starting to see that it was a life worth fighting for.

It's now 2015, and my life is better, richer, fuller than I ever could have imagined. I have sturdy friendships, a wonderful marriage, and a fulfilling career, and I don't wake up wanting to die every day.

I work as a peer support specialist and a peer coordinator for a community mental health organization. I stumbled into the field by checking out nonprofit online job listings, not sure of what I'd find. I'd wanted to work in the mental health field since I was a kid, but I thought that having an extensive psych history took me out of the running. But here, in this job description, "lived experience receiving mental health services" was a requirement! A degree wasn't required, clinical experience wasn't required—only my experiences and my willingness to share them. Seeing this job description felt eerily similar to seeing my diagnosis in the *DSM* all those years ago. It seemed written just for me. I had found a new home.

I have since passed the exam to become a certified peer specialist. Working in this field, training in this field, and meeting other people in this field have really helped me reframe my experiences.

I no longer believe that everyone has to get better the exact same way I have. But I do have to believe that there is a path to recovery for everyone. My job as a peer specialist is to communicate hope. I can imagine how valuable it would have been, when I was at my worst, to have the opportunity to work with someone who had been there and was on the other side. When I struggled, I had to create that hope for myself that there even *was* an "other side." I wouldn't be where I am if I had stopped believing that was a possibility.

The word HOPE is now tattooed across my arm, over spots where I used to cut myself. Hope for myself and continuing to build a better life is what sustains me. And now I get to share that hope with others and empower them to sustain themselves. I am the luckiest person I know.

7. If I Were to Tell You That I Have a Disorder That Affects Only 2 Percent of the Population, What Would Your Reaction Be?

I was diagnosed with borderline personality disorder in 2013—a mental illness that kills one in ten of those affected. According to my knowledge, BPD is one of the most misunderstood and often stigmatized mental health conditions.

It all began in high school; I felt like an outsider and a young girl who didn't quite fit in with her peers. I was different, to put it bluntly. I liked all the wrong sorts of things, listened to the wrong music, dressed the wrong way, and hardly spoke. Being bullied was a part of my routine whilst in high school. In grade nine, I began having a horrendous pain in my abdomen, and when I went to my mum, she said, "Don't worry. Just take an Advil." Months passed, and the pain didn't subside, and I kept on insisting that I had pain, but all I would get was the same reaction: take an Advil. Eventually my mum began noticing how thin I was becoming, and that was an alert for her. I dared not eat, because the pain only intensified when I ate. When she finally took me to the hospital, I got many tests run, and they all came out negative. Nothing seemed to show any cause for concern, except for the fact that

I was rail-thin and my abdomen felt as if it were on fire. Eventually I saw a specialist at the Children's Hospital, where I was told I was an attention-seeking teenager who was anorexic and sent immediately to see a psychologist. This greatly affected me, because I felt so invalidated. All I wanted was for the pain to go away, but rather than going away, it only intensified and my heart grew sad. After months of seeing this psychologist, she gave the report that my pain was very much real. Truth of the matter was I had adhesions, and all it took was a simple procedure to remove them.

But after that event, I began hearing a voice in my head, a voice that kept on telling me how good I looked when I was thin. And I noticed all the attention I was getting at school and all these compliments that were thrown my way. It kind of felt good. So I began to become more conscious of my weight and how much I was putting into my body.

I also distanced myself more from friends and family, finding comfort and solace in my own solitude. As the voice turned into two voices which began to get more destructive in what they were saying, I felt a panic rise in me. All this negativity was being thrown my way, and I had nowhere to escape from it. School was a nightmare, although no one could see I was suffering, and my friends had absolutely no idea that I was being teased and tortured during class. At home, my voices would torment me, and I just wanted it all to stop.

"Do it. You know you want to," I heard at 4:00 a.m. I had this intense urge to just take a razor and cut myself. And with the encouragement of the voices, I did. A sense of relief and euphoria rose in my blood and awoke all my senses. I felt so much better.

I found my comfort.

Three years later, I gave the impression of the good, happy girl, when in truth my heart was withering away. Depression would overtake me, and I fought so hard to push it aside, but I just couldn't do so any longer. I didn't have the strength to go on pretending. I was hearing around twenty voices at this point, all with the same initial goal: to kill me. I dared not tell anyone, because I didn't want to be another nuisance, another stressor. But I just couldn't take it any longer, so I wrote a good-bye note and took forty Tylenol pills, hoping I would fall asleep and never wake up.

Next thing I knew, I was staring at a bright light. I wondered to myself if I was in heaven, but no, I was in the hospital, with an IV strapped to my arm. I had *failed*. I was admitted to the adolescent psychiatric unit later that day and spent a month there. In an attempt to ease my heartache, sense of failure, desire to die, and extreme sadness, I found ways to self-harm—my only means of coping. Pencils, my nails, wood chips, anything. Finding a way of self-harming is always easy. Anything can be used.

On a scale of 1 to 10, how do you feel? On a scale of 1 to 10, how suicidal are you? On a scale of 1 to 10, on a scale of 1 to 10, on a scale of 1 to 10—I was sick and tired of hearing the same repetitive questions being asked over and over again. My psychiatrist at the time gave me a questionnaire, and upon reading the questions, it was as if I were reading exactly how I felt. Questions about feeling empty, about getting bouts of anger, about engaging in self-harm/suicidal behaviors, about being afraid that others would abandon me, about how my view of others could shift dramatically. "You, my dear, have what is called borderline personality disorder," my psychiatrist said to me in a very calm voice.

My journey didn't end there. I self-harmed so many times that my body is now adorned with over three hundred scars. I attempted suicide more than five times. I ran away from home on countless occasions. I would yell and throw things in the house. I had the police show up at my house three times to take me to the hospital. I was hospitalized more than ten times and tried to run away from the ward. The voices grew to hundreds, which would drive me to bouts of insanity. I had a feeding tube down my nose. I would sign up on dating sites and meet up with strange men, causing me to get raped. I would steal. I would have panic attacks. I would drink bleach. I would starve myself. I would binge and purge. It was a mess. I was a mess. A living nightmare.

What has kept me here is the support of my family. Through everything I have put them through, they still stayed and held my hand. I went through intense therapy that felt like a waste of time, but eventually, over a long and tedious process, I began to find answers. I am not better yet, but I am more stable. As my therapist once told me, "Two steps forward, one step back, but you're always moving forward." And there is truth in that. Relapse is a part of recovery. It's hard to believe that's true when you're living it, but at the end of the day, if you are still on this earth, you have made progress.

I'm no expert on relationships, but I can tell you that being in one when dealing with BPD is a roller coaster ride. If my boyfriend complimented me, I took it as sarcasm; if he was rude, I took it as a great personal attack. He is the person closest to me, yet I feel like he's the enemy. Your feelings go from extreme love to extreme hatred. From needing to be held to needing to be left alone. It's not easy on your partner and can often lead to a bad ending, which was the case for me. My boyfriend told me he could no longer be in a relationship with me, because I was too much to handle. He was afraid of my impulsivity, and when I put him through the fright of an overdose attempt, it made him realize he wasn't strong enough to be my support. I felt like a fool for believing that someone was capable of loving me. I felt as is no one in their right mind would ever love me. I thought that had I been prettier, smarter, better in bed, more talkative, and not "crazy," I wouldn't have driven him away.

But maybe I'm wrong, because I know I'm not the only one living with BPD, and I've read biographies on those who have lived with BPD and had successful relationships.

Living with borderline personality disorder is one hell of a ride. It's hard, it's scary, it's passionate, it's angry, and it's everything in between. But when you're given the right coping tools and a safety plan and a structure, life becomes more doable. Don't give up. And don't let it win, because when you come through to the other side, you see the world in a different perspective.

8. Restoration

It was only a matter of time before I was not able to make it through another day. Some symptoms of borderline personality disorder began in early childhood and worsened as I developed and got older. What seemed like sadness to others would send me into a black hole of despair and emptiness. What seemed like a small embarrassment to others would send me into a whirlpool of shame, humiliation, and anxiety. What seemed to simply bother others would send me into intense, convulsing panic or anger. It was as if my brain would instantly kick into overdrive the moment any external stimulations crossed me. I would perceive a neutral expression as anger or hostility toward me, which would cause me to become frightened and overwhelmed by paranoia. Periodically, a small comment from someone would keep me from sleeping for days, if not weeks. I was drowned by self-hatred that would get reinforced by these perceptions and reactions from my hypersensitivity. Complete anguish filled the rest of the gaps inside of me. As a result of my difficulties, day-to-day tasks were debilitating for me to try to accomplish. My insides seemed to shrivel away and turn to ashes before I could even get out of bed in the morning. Oftentimes, the intense stress and anxiety would provoke hallucinations and even stress-triggered seizures. The haunting voices in my head transformed into little whispers or laughs during times of perceived failure. At other times, the intensity would often cause dissociation, an extreme disconnection from reality, as if it were my brain's way of trying to protect me from any more pain. This included severe drifting away, unresponsiveness, trouble with my memory, and a numb, empty dream-like floating sensation. In response to triggers, I would become firmly detached from myself and my surroundings. As an attempt to relieve all this turmoil, I began self-destructive behaviors at age ten, if not sooner.

My condition worsened as time went on. How I was able to see through my tears and find my way to the nearest bathroom at times, I am not sure. The intensity from crying often made me sick to my stomach. My only option in high school was to pull all-nighters every single night, as I had severe difficulty trying to fall asleep. Nightmares took over the times I would rarely fall asleep and have the chance to be at peace. If I did fall asleep, I would crash until around midnight the next day, out of exhaustion from my emotions. Eventually, I transferred to high school online, so I could attempt to sleep. I suddenly made the choice to get enrolled in thirteen classes at once, to graduate two years early. This was an attempt to fill the void inside of me and experience some sort of self-worth, as I realized I had no sense of self. My goals, future, and entire life were all based off of the exact present moment to me, which changed daily. To me, if I wasn't unrealistically achieving major accomplishments (like finishing an entire class in one day with an A), I was useless, meaningless, and not appropriate to the world. It was as if my mind were demanding me to achieve perfectionism every day, or it would punish me. This struggle quickly escalated. Most of my days were spent not even being able to tell who I was if I looked in the mirror. Periodically, I could have sworn the person staring back at me did something different from what I was actually doing. I had no idea who and what I seemed to be. I felt foreign. I felt like an alien from a different planet.

When I joined martial arts when I was twelve years old, it was the one factor in my life that kept me going. I put my entire heart into it and wanted to continue living for something. I gained a sense of self and watched myself do movements that I did not know I would ever be able to do. For the first time ever, I had something in my life that belonged to me. The hypersensitivity extended to all areas of my life, including positive emotions at times. I was frequently overpowered by intense euphoria, passion, and contentment; nonetheless, it did not take long for me to experience symptoms of perfectionism, anxiety, depression, and self-hatred, which affected me in my practice. Finally, one month before it was time to test for my black belt, I had a sudden, immense downfall in my life as a result of long-term abuse and maltreatment. I was not able to test for my black belt and no longer was in class. For three days straight, I did not leave my bed. I had dealt with suicidal ideations most of my life, but it intensified in that time. Dramatic pictures of ways to escape the pain flashed through my head and subdued my dreams. I lost the only positive aspect I had in my life. I lost what I lived for.

Three days of lying in my bed, completely devastated, dragged on to what felt like an entire month. At the last moment, everything turned around, when someone decided to step in. A magnificent martial arts master who was aware of my struggles reached out after he heard about what had happened to me. He was also a skilled mental health worker, one whom others would often turn to for work advice and treatment plans. From the start, we easily connected and became very close friends. He became my new master, tested me for my black belt at my original time, and certified me as an instructor. Additionally, he gave me eleven martial arts books and two DVDs to enjoy and learn from. All of this was done for me without any cost. After much mistreatment and disregard toward me in my life, I was absolutely astounded by his wisdom and care for me. Opening up to someone was difficult, because of such experiences, but I had never been happier in my life for doing so. I realized someone had gone out of their way to find me, after hearing I was lost and broken, exclusively to help me and care for me. That meant more to me than anything in my life.

After months of extensive assessment and getting to know him, he began to explain to me why I struggled so deeply and experienced the wide range of symptoms that I do—I have borderline personality disorder. This was not the first time I was told that I displayed the condition, but it was the first time I considered and accepted it. As he explained to me what it was, what was happening to me, and why, everything started to make sense. My hypersensitivity and my inability to regulate the intensity led to symptoms in all areas of my life, with my emotions, patterns of thinking, behavior, and perception. At last, I had some insight into what was happening to me and was on my way to recovery. We began coping strategies that would help me identify rooted feelings and complications and cope with them. Coincidentally, he also admitted to having BPD and told me of similar struggles he had. The mixture of our intensity, similar hardships, and passion for martial arts strengthened our relationship and care for each other even more. In addition to his being my mentor and dear friend, I saw he could understand and was able to help me with martial arts as well as recovery, personal growth, and development. I was not alone, and I never had to be again. He eventually told me I was family to him and that he wanted to protect me and loved me. As he was also a writer, he wrote a beautiful dedication to me in one of his martial arts books he was revising. Although I continued to struggle greatly, he was always there to be my best friend, help me, and guide me. He saved my life. I do not say that lightly.

Until one day, I could not breathe. The horrible news shot through me like a bullet, and I almost dropped to the floor, unable to feel my arms and legs. Sweat was dripping down my body as I sat down, shaking uncontrollably. It was as if poison were running through my veins, slowly heightening my emotions, until it fed off of every positive thought and feeling before completely devouring me. BPD reactions like this were nothing new to me; however, this time, my martial arts master, hero, mentor, and close father figure had just taken his life. Intense reactions to abandonment and grief took over me. I immediately felt like I had not only lost the most significant person in my life but also lost a huge portion of my enthusiasm, soul, and identity. We had plans to eventually move closer to each other, teach martial arts together, and train every day while continuing recovery. It all ended in a second. The passion and life in my eyes left the moment it left his. Before I even knew he had taken his last breath, I felt it happen.

The intense torment of losing a tremendous part of me still influences my life to this day. It has been a little over a year now since my master passed. Borderline personality disorder has made this situation dreadfully hard to cope with, and I unfortunately still struggle with the condition regularly. It is like being on a thin piece of glass that breaks down and shatters with the slightest touch. Every day, I work on carefully putting the sharp pieces back together somehow. If my master hadn't found me, I would have had no idea where to begin. Although he may not be here physically, he guides me often and continues to make an impact. Every burning tear that runs down my face is soothed by the memory of him. I cannot begin to imagine how my life would have ended up without him. He showed me there is a reason for me to be here and helped me discover some strength I didn't know I had. Daily, I reflect on all the many different words he said to me. In his book dedication to me, my master stated, "When life hands you something that is hard to swallow, tough to deal with, and painful to overcome, you remember all the sweat and effort it took to get here. What miraculous ripples we cause when we refuse to give up, back down, or be made less by life's challenges… We can't help but affect the people we know (most often without even directly trying), and in some way and on some level, I know I am a better and stronger person for having been privileged enough to learn about the strength you've shown in your relatively short life thus far." Although I may not always be able to see it through the intense darkness of BPD, perhaps I impact more individuals than I realize. Every day is an accomplishment to overcome being clouded by such a condition, and the strength it takes is unthinkable. Borderline personality disorder may cloud my emotions, thinking, and behavior, but it cannot and will not cloud my potential.

9. Trust No One

For my entire life, I have lived by the code of one distinct mantra: "Trust no one."

I started therapy when I was fourteen, after being hospitalized for a severe eating disorder that nearly ended my life. Since then, therapists have been an intermittent constant in my life, with many wounded and fallen in their midst, but I do remember my first real breakthrough, when I was about twenty-four, which helped explain my overwhelming and inexplicable inability to trust. It stemmed back to a particular event when my sister and I (aged eight and six, respectively) each had a friend over for a playdate, and she decided that it would be fun for all of us to participate in one of her favorite games: "beauty parlor." Cathy and her guest took my friend Miranda into the bathroom first, locking me out, so I went to my bedroom to await my turn. Several minutes later, Miranda came out with wet hair and a tear-streaked face to coldly tell me, "I don't want to be your friend anymore. I hate you."

I was stunned and perplexed. I had no idea what I had done to make her decide out of the blue that she *hated* me. My first real friend and the girl I spent all of my time with had decided that I was so awful, through no doing of my own, that I was no longer worthy of her friendship. She spent the last few hours of our playdate with my older sister and her friend, instead, while I sat alone in my room to try to figure out what I had done to make her leave.

Back at school the next day, away from the grasp of my sister, we made up, and I found out the real reason behind what had happened. Cathy, while washing Miranda's beautiful long hair, had held her head under the running water and refused to let her up for air until she agreed to no longer be friends with me. My sister had been torturing me both physically and mentally as far back as I could remember (the story of her stuffing me in a little red toy chest and sitting on top until I was practically out of air comes to mind), but now her attacks were including the few allies I had made, and her methods were forceful.

In that instant, I learned at a very young age that anyone can and will turn on you in a second. No one could be trusted, especially not my sister.

She got a light slap on the hand from my parents for what she had done, once I told them, but the punishment was neither an appropriate acknowledgment of the emotional damage she had caused nor severe enough to deter her from similar actions in the future. I was left to cope and fend for myself from there on out.

Everything was chalked up to sibling rivalry. Cathy was a very unhappy, overweight child who took out her aggression on me, and those occurrences escalated as we got older. Her favorite times to lash out were when she had an audience, so school was the perfect platform. Another notable period in my life was when we switched to a private school where we had to ride a van with other commuting children. For forty-five minutes every morning, I would be subjected to constant ridicule at the hands of Cathy while the other children laughed at me. I would enter the school with swollen eyes and spend the first half of the day with my head down while I waited for my tears to subside, and then it was back on the van for another forty-five minute ride-of-hell home. The ways in which she publicly berated and privately abused me lasted until she left for college, and even when she came home to visit, it continued. No one stood up for me, and no one intervened.

After that, every relationship or friendship I had became a test. Unaware of why I was doing it, I acted out in every possible way to see how much the person on the receiving end could take before they decided I wasn't worth the effort. The closer I became to people, the harder I pushed, and every person who disowned me reinforced my method of destruction. I needed to make people prove they were going to stick with me, no matter what, but I couldn't accept love, because I hated myself too much. The only person I could rely on was me, because I was the only one who couldn't leave. I had no experience with trusting anyone in my world.

The first time I tried to kill myself, I was ten years old. It wasn't a serious attempt, merely wrapping a small pink belt with heart-shaped cutouts around my neck and pulling tight to see how closing off my circulation would feel, but I knew that I was depressed and I didn't want to live the life I had. I withdrew from my family and used my isolation to fill my head with literature and film and music, things that would later make me seem interesting and good with conversation: a distraction. I studied dark, complicated characters, people I felt an affinity toward because they also hurt inside, and I secretly tried on different personalities. I paid close attention to my classmates as they played out their teenage drama, and I took silent note of what made people tick. I padded the empty loneliness I had inside with all of these things, turning myself into a patchwork Frankenstein of a person, who could relate to everyone and no one at all. My interactions with people became a predatory game of cat and mouse, using the interesting persona that I had cultivated over time to draw them in, only to turn into an abuser myself and push them back out. I became a monster.

I also acquired a lengthy list of vices, as I learned that getting in trouble meant both obtaining my parents' attention and feeding the dark hole inside of me. The aforementioned eating disorder was very effective in both ways and grew to an obsession that shut out everything else in my life. Once that was "dealt" with, I graduated to substance abuse. My burgeoning relationship with alcohol far exceeded the high doses of Prozac that my mother was monitoring my consumption of each morning, and every dance I had with it led me farther and farther down the hole. Much like Alice with the "Drink Me" elixir, I could disappear or become larger than life, depending on which need was stronger. The obvious next steps were to commingle all of this with some very dangerous and destructive relationships, to keep cutting off every hope I had to learn to trust. There was no happy ending, only happiness ending.

Through all of these occurrences, I realized I needed a reason for why relationships fail. Friends grow apart, lovers leave, family members neglect or disown; all of these relationships in my mind are doomed, and I want to be able to give it a reason. I don't want someone to come to me and tell me they hate me without a reason, so I give them one. I give them lots of reasons. I keep giving them reasons until one of them sticks, and though I'm upset when they can't take it anymore, I can rationalize why it happened and find some comfort in that. If I take matters into my own hands and do it to myself, I can come full circle with accepting the blame, to feed my inexplicable need to feel worthless. I am in control of my pain, and no one else is. But most of all, I don't have to face my fear of getting attached and depending on someone, only to have them come to me down the road and tell me that they're leaving. That is a pain that I just cannot bear.

There have been many attempts at "normalizing" over the years. One person I pushed and pushed until he broke is an ex-boyfriend of mine whom I still remain friends with almost five years after the fact (a long time for someone to stick around in my world). He was gorgeous, and we had instant chemistry, and I did what I always do. I pulled him in with the interesting, unique, manic magnetism that I have harnessed over the years. As soon as that great first date, I climbed back behind my wall and peered over the top, pushing bricks out, little by little, to fall on his head and see how much he could take. That lack of self-esteem I was still trying to patch between the empty holes, coupled with my old habits of pushing people away, meant that I was nowhere near ready for what he was willing to offer: a person I could trust. At one point, my lack of self-esteem even convinced me that he was dating me as a joke, that maybe he was playing some game, where he would earn points for banging a chubby chick. I thought he was silently laughing at me the whole time, and it undermined my every movement. He seemed like a genuinely nice, grounded person, and he was interested in me, which made me trust him the least.

It only took a few weeks, maybe a month at most, before I had buried him in bricks and he couldn't take me anymore. I hastened to bring back the "cool, fun" persona, pretending that it was a momentary lapse of sanity, and drew him back in for a second round. This one lasted even less time, as I tested his own invisible fence for weaknesses and then poked my fingers through the hole to prod him. The last straw was as crude and immature as discovering his extreme distaste for littering and shoving trash out of his car window as he drove me home. I was desperate to get him away from me because I was falling for him, so that was my reaction.

Our relationship picked up again once I moved to another city a few hundred miles away. He had passed the first test of chasing an undesirable, and this was a more satisfactory position for me to start letting my guard down, because in my years, I have learned that I need a lot of space to feel comfortable. A *lot*. If I could meet someone from across the country, and we could slowly walk from rest stop to rest stop, while mailing each other lengthy, handwritten letters, it would probably be the ideal way for me to start a relationship. As a loner who has learned to depend only on herself, I can articulate best through the written word. If you put me in front of an actual human being and ask me to put down my weapons and start taking off the armor, alcohol is the only fissure you'll find. Very few people would describe me as a shy or anxious person, because I've become a master illusionist when it comes to hiding my feelings, but that's exactly what I am.

I spent a long time hiding in bottles and pills and drugs to keep the fun, happy, high Katie appealing to those around her. The downside to that was that I could never keep it up for long enough, and eventually fun, happy, high Katie would push it too far and spiral down into miserable, emotional, angry, aggressive Katie, faster than you can say Jameson. The more I have stepped away from using alcohol as an emotional scapegoat and edged my way closer to sobriety and self-actualization, the more I realize just how long I have been hiding from myself and everyone else.

Making observations like this after all the years of suppressing, doubting, and overanalyzing everything and anything that surfaced is similar to a person who has broken their leg and is in so much physical pain that they pass out. My body's automatic response to getting too close to a nerve is to shut down. My brain doesn't want to visit the emotional storm that is always stuffed way down deep. That emotional storm leaves a lot of wreckage in its wake when it surfaces, and I'm still learning to maneuver the direction of its path so that it doesn't wipe out entire populations of people who are living around the edges of my world.

I was diagnosed with BPD at the age of twenty by the first therapist I ever managed to trust. We started working together when I was about sixteen, and I returned to seeing her when I hit a long period of depression that rendered me incapable of taking care of myself. My therapist told me that she had suspected all along that I had borderline personality disorder, but couldn't diagnose me until I was eighteen. Having a label and a clinical understanding of why I was "the way I was" opened up a vein of relief in me. I finally had an identity.

Since then, life has been a series of ups and downs on a merry-go-round that spins a little slower every year. I've moved to several cities and poked and prodded hundreds of people in my attempt to learn how to form healthy relationships. Most of those experiments are failed, but with age and therapy, I am learning how to release emotion in a healthy, acceptable way, instead of the torrential explosions that result from trying to handle everything on my own. It often feels like purgatory, because I'm always stuck between the past and the present, on a loop. Much like this essay, nothing ever feels finished, because there is no definitive rehabilitation for people with BPD. Only maintenance.

I am still very confused about how to interact with the rest of the world, and I'm doing my best to learn how to make sense of things, without the coping skills that most were equipped with during their formative years. There is one thing I take pride in, and that is that I am unlike anyone else you'll ever meet in this lifetime. In learning about my own personal shortcomings, I have become a sort of honorary therapist. I have used that insight to build a career helping others understand undesirable behavior and how much it relates to their own personality traits. I found a way to turn my dark existence into a light for others, and that is the best feeling I have ever experienced. It has helped me realize that I'm worth something and that I have an ability to communicate with others who are misunderstood and incapable of vocalizing their exact needs.

There is still hope for all of us.

10. Just Like a Timepiece

To the right of me sat Natalie Portman. To the left of me sat the Crown Prince of Dubai. In front of me stood our Nobel laureate professor. And between them, I sat, holding within me the most infamous personality of all, my borderline personality disorder.

I was Mexican-American and a student at Harvard University, the oldest and most prestigious academic institution in the country, established in 1636. Only a small percentage of applicants are admitted, and a fraction of those are Hispanic like me. It is an environment that will test every fiber of your being and push you beyond the logical limits of a mind you once believed you possessed. It is not for the faint of heart.

My arrival to Harvard and Cambridge, Massachusetts, in 2000 was not unlike the experience of others. First came the initial shock of being assigned twenty-five books to read per class by the end of the semester. Second came the sudden realization that there was no one, nowhere, who would provide guidance on these subjects. Whereas once we each competed in our high schools to be valedictorians, and just about every Harvard student graduated a valedictorian of their respective high school, we realized we were now to compete not with each other but with ourselves.

And so began the fight within me.

The symptoms of my borderline personality disorder had surfaced at a far earlier age. I was fourteen and young and isolated. I sat alone in the middle school cafeteria every day, feeling intensely ashamed of how unlikeable I must appear to others. Each day, as we filed into the cafeteria, I would feel a brief spark of hope that someone would ask me to sit at their table.

At night, I would run my hand across the pale smoothness of my underarm and trace the faint blue veins. I would hold a tiny metal cog with biting edges from a clock I had disassembled out of curiosity against my skin. Then I would pull it against my skin over and over in neat parallel lines. I had an affinity for neatness and aesthetics. I was an artist and a scientist. And in this case, I was making art of my skin, and unrelenting, brutal pain was my medium. I felt a calmness I would learn to seek over and over and in more forms than this one.

The cutting continued. It became more extravagant while I made certain it remained hidden from anyone. It was the only friend I had. But I was a straight-A student with awards in every academic subject and an all-star athlete. There was nothing wrong with me. How could there be? I was just being silly.

A year later, I became suicidal. I yearned for an escape. At night, during sweaty nightmares, I would restlessly push the covers off me and imagine the rest that would come from finally killing myself. The do-it, don't-do-it theme became my desktop wallpaper, again, for years and years to come.

In spectacular fashion, I pulled off graduating as our high school valedictorian with admittance to Harvard. Underneath, however, in the bottomless trough that no one bothered to notice because everyone was looking up in awe, ran the crisis of myself. I was suicidal, I was cutting several times a day, and I had begun alternating between extreme anorexia and bulimia. I was invisible to the world, it appeared. I was a commodity valued for my mind.

I drank night after night at Harvard without stopping. And each night I blacked out. This was not the usual college partying. It often ended in the emergency room with my blood alcohol content at its near limits. What I sought on those nights was a complete dissociation from my experience. I wanted to run farther from myself than I had run before. And like every high achiever, I was going to do it, and do it better than anyone had ever done it before. That was to include shoplifting.

In total, among books, malls, and stores, I was arrested four times, with four felony counts of theft. The short nights and hours I spent in jail waiting to be released on bail were sickening. The fluorescent lights swirled in my eyes, and I sat as far from the military wool blankets as I could. I hate wool. I find it intolerable as a material.

After the fourth arrest, the judge reviewed my background and considered my case. In exchange for leniency, the judge requested that I be placed in full-time therapy. It was clear that I was unfit to return to Harvard. My parents were beyond appalled. Their little girl had entirely evaporated.

I initiated a formal leave of absence and, after evaluation by the university's health services, was recommended to visit a dialectical behavior therapy treatment center in the city. I read the diagnosis of borderline personality disorder in the

DSM-IV. I bit my lip. There I was. In black and white and Times New Roman.

In the days that followed, I entered the treatment center with freshly burnt skin. I had begun burning myself shortly before, my new form of painful expression. It hurt maddeningly, and I was well equipped for whatever this center might ask of me. No one would hurt me.

I was weary and folded up tightly. The center was pleasantly decorated with soft yellow walls, geometric pillows, watercolors of innocent birds, and rooms labeled and distinguished by nautical flags. I met with a few unmemorable psychiatrists and revealed nothing about myself other than what was neatly printed on the forms before them. However, one doctor in particular—Dr. Dunn—took an alternate approach. He disarmed me over the course of several meetings. I did not weep my miseries at his feet. I never cried, actually. That was something particular about me. But I did feel a thread of understanding between this man with a mustache and two glass elephants on his coffee table and me.

He made it clear that he would be available to me at any time of day or night. At any minute. All I needed to do was page him and he would be there for me in the moments when I was going to harm myself. I was filled with fear.

About a month into the program, he asked me to allow our session to be watched through a two-way mirror by a large group of postdoctoral students. I agreed. As we sat there, he said about my suicidality, "You're afraid of living." Perhaps he was being didactic, but in that moment, any trust he had established with me died. I was hurt beyond measure. I felt betrayed. If I could choose to feel differently, I would. My pain rushed to the surface, and all I wanted in that moment was to die. No one could make me feel safe. Not even this man who had said he would "be there" for me. When would this end? When would the broken Christmas lights finally turn back on?

I shuffled my feet through the dirt and continued with the DBT program, learning skills here and there, but feeling vastly alone and no better off than when I had arrived. I had the indirect prestige of knowing I was working with the "best adolescent DBT therapist" on the East Coast and perhaps in the United States. But I never told him the truth. There was the understanding between us that I was suicidal and self-harming. That I must show up for my appointments. But it ended there. I attempted suicide by overdosing on two separate occasions. In one, the hotel maid happened upon me while turning down the sheets for the evening. In the other, I made myself sick as a dog by taking Lithium and an antiemetic.

My relationships with others were either nonexistent or supremely fragile. For as long as I could remember, I yearned for this unknown, indefinable someone who would arrive and know me, understand me for exactly who I was, who would take the pain away, and who would guide me to a richer life of meaning. That was a child's fantasy, not unlike my childhood fantasy of living in Disney World during the winters in Maine while my family was inundated by snow.

In June 2003, a fresh group of postdoctoral students arrived at the center to continue learning and provide services to the clients. The severity of my behaviors called for a supporting therapist in addition to Dr. Dunn. And so began the most profound and meaningful relationship of my entire life.

I was shy and always looked down at my shoes. She listened and drew from me the most painful thoughts and feelings I held within me. There was something about the two of us that simply clicked. I'd had enough therapy in my time to know that the bond between therapist and client cannot be forced. It is binary. It either exists or doesn't. It thrives over time with trust and vulnerability. I had never been so connected to anyone in my life. In fact, I had never been securely attached to anyone in my life in the first place.

Bolstered by Dr. Chase, I began making plans at the start of 2004 to reenter Harvard in the fall. But it was in June 2004 when my heart broke. Dr. Chase shared that her one-year postdoctoral program with the treatment center had ended, and she was now leaving Boston to continue her specialization in DBT. If hope had an anti-Christ, this was it. Everything that I had planned for, the traction that began forming beneath me, suddenly ceased. I could not believe it. I did not cry. It was fine. I folded the pain away neatly like a handkerchief. She gave me a journal to express my feelings over her leaving. I left it blank. And on the last days, we said our good-byes. I did not cry.

After her abandonment, I reentered Harvard, graduated successfully, and also graduated an expert in cocaine addiction, crack, ecstasy, Ritalin, marijuana, and sexual hedonism. I threw myself into these as balms for the pain of abandonment. My life felt like a snake eating its own tail. I was not in therapy yet worked in prestigious, high-paying jobs, mimicking my past dissonances.

This lasted seven years. I have no idea how I survived or had even the semblance of humanity. I was a monster inside. And I hated every cell within me.

At the end of the seven years, a job opportunity led me to relocate to a new city. Compounded by geographic disorientation, my suicidal urges skyrocketed, and I made plans to purchase a gun, once and for all. My desktop wallpaper still displayed the do-it, don't-do-it theme, so I often walked into gun stores, held my breath, and turned back around in a daze. At times, I would hold a shotgun in my hand, pretending to the clerk that it was for "sport." Or I would buy a box of shells and store them in my nightstand.

In the late spring of 2013, I discovered that my former therapist was living in the same city as me. I did not cry.

I started to draft an e-mail. "Hi," I wrote. Then I sat there for a long while with my chin in hand. Would she even remember me? Surely not. "Hi, Dr. Chase," I managed to get down. I erred on the side of formality, introduced myself as I would if I were meeting the president of a large corporation, clipped any emotion from my words, and ended with a leap akin to crossing the Black Cavern Chasm. I asked her if she was seeing clients, and if so, would she be willing to see me? As the Greeks once told us, desperate times call for desperate measures. I attached what was left of my seared heart to the e-mail and sent it.

Two days later, she responded. With exclamation points, to boot, and the recognition of me I feared she had lost. Of course, she would see me, she said. The emptiness inside shook slightly. I did not cry. Seven entire years had passed. Never would I have thought the only person I had ever truly loved and felt safe with, the only person who could possibly save me from myself, would reenter my life by some roll of the dice.

And as on the first day we met, I looked down at my shoes. My shame filled her small office, and she gently asked that I look at her. So I did. She showed me in her eyes that she held no judgment of me. If there were ever a remedy for the ill effects of borderline personality disorder, it is DBT. But DBT alone does not suffice, as I learned many years ago. A framework without a heart and a soul is nothing. For DBT to truly work, there must be a therapist who is truly committed from her heart and soul to the recovery of her client. Dr. Chase has always given her heart and soul.

Dr. Chase and I worked as a team through the darkest days of my suicidal urges, taking my desperate calls at all hours of the day and night, and she stood by me on the occasion when I did purchase a gun and returned it. I am no longer suicidal. She quelled and finally extinguished the fire that was causing me to self-harm. I no longer cut or burn myself. I am no longer a drug addict. She researched the latest behavioral strategies for treating eating disorders, strategically approaching each facet with an intelligence, compassion, and determination that has led to my recovery. As each disorder has been eliminated, one by one, Dr. Chase and I have now turned our attention to the underlying causes that fuel these behaviors: the emotional traumas of my life. Through the behavioral method of prolonged exposure therapy, we have begun the excruciating process of unraveling these moments and providing me with the opportunity to confirm whether my worst fears are justified.

Dr. Chase and I continue to meet twice a week at the time of this writing. She is by far the most important person in my life. She has done more for me than anyone else I have ever known. There are still moments when I struggle, and she is available to me at any moment, both day and night. The diagnosis of borderline personality disorder is not an excuse for me. It is simply an explanation. I have begun to tentatively form friendships, although many times I still retreat within the safety of myself. The other day I found myself saying "I like myself."

And I cry now.

11. Breaking Bad

I was diagnosed with BPD nine months after I gave birth to my fourth child. I had been married for about ten years. We had our ups and downs and were in and out of marriage counseling. Our problems were attributed to both of our abusive childhoods. I was first diagnosed with PCOS after my first child was born, at the age of nineteen. PCOS is a hormonal imbalance that affected me in many ways, including weight gain, moodiness, and irregular cycles. My husband was angry and afraid I would not be able to have any more children, and so he immediately took me to a doctor, and I began fertility treatment to make sure I would be pregnant with another child right away, as we were told this condition would worsen with age and is associated with infertility. The hormones and treatments were a struggle.

I was on and off Zoloft for depression and postpartum depression. Somehow I kept a few jobs over the years and raised the kids with relatively minor issues. Or so I thought. I didn't realize that I would make excuses for many of the things I was doing. I tried to keep everything in the house super clean and be a calm mother who never raised her voice and had a three-course dinner every night. When the children did something good, I would make a big deal of it, thinking how wonderful I was for the positive reinforcement, when really I was going way overboard. Whether it was buying big gifts or making a lavish party, I was not able to gauge properly the appropriateness. It wasn't just with them. If I would see cereal on sale, I wouldn't buy one box but would buy twenty and always have a reason why and justify it. If I thought it was appropriate to get a little cleaning help in the house, I wouldn't take two hours; I would take twenty. Whenever I would cook, I would double or triple the recipe, whether I needed it or not. I was always prepared for everything, and there was nothing I didn't have.

I lived like that, seemingly okay for a while. It was exhausting. It wasn't until I stopped nursing my fourth child that I just couldn't juggle it anymore. I was trying to do everything for everyone, and I never knew when to stop. I also was trying to have everything just so perfect. It was very extreme.

I don't know if it was the hormonal change that pushed me over the edge. Truth is, I hadn't been able to bounce back after my third child's birth. Taking care of the kids and house became too difficult. I stopped showering and didn't want to get dressed. I was sluggish, tired, moody, antisocial, and slowly withdrawing. I began to sleep quite a bit and then suddenly had terrible insomnia. I thought I was hearing things and was talking to myself. I could tell I was losing touch with reality.

I was hospitalized for about ten days, briefly released as an outpatient, and back in the hospital a few days later for another week.

That hospitalization came with the harsh diagnosis, BPD. It scared my husband and parents a great deal. I began DBT therapy. I was doing well and started working again. I had begun to deal with the issue but couldn't really balance anything. I had another relapse about a year later, and at that point my husband filed for divorce, not being able to live with my instability. I had become almost manic and was working a ton. I started two new businesses and was working full-time. I can't pinpoint what it was, but I felt off. I had lost a sense of my boundaries in so many ways, especially socially.

It was easy to say we divorced over this, but the truth is my husband, himself, just a few months after we wed, disclosed he suffered from social anxiety and on-and-off depression. He would be on and off Zoloft, Xanax, Klonopin, drinking, and smoking pot to deal with it. His ups and downs clashed with mine from very early on. We married young and had babies very quickly, which was just the way it had to be, as orthodox Jews married off young, via a matchmaker. He was the first boy I met, and I jumped in very quickly. We met eight times before becoming engaged and were married three months later. Without much, we just started life and worked tirelessly to build an empire. With only high school educations under our belts, we somehow managed to build a successful, multi-million-dollar business and were living "the good life." It was too good when it got good and came with too much stress and no time for us. We tried to balance things out. We both worked hard.

As with my diagnosis of PCOS, my husband was angry and took on the BPD, wanting to fix everything and make me perfect. He would control me and micromanage my therapists and medications, in essence sabotaging whatever work or progress I was to make. He would say that using skills like lotion or crosswords to relax was for crazy people, and he would take away the lotion or rip up my book.

He was so afraid of the diagnosis, he didn't want me turning into what the books said I might…so he decided that keeping me busy and forcing me to be "normal" would make things right.

I wasn't getting better at all. I was trying to find my way and nurture myself, but the demands he and the family pushed on me, intentionally or not, were not allowing me to recover and balance myself. My husband had also interfered with my medications, saying he didn't think I needed it all, so he would take some of my pills. Then he would say I needed more medication and threaten to hospitalize me to get reevaluated if I wouldn't shape up. To him, that meant getting a job. There were so many changes up and down in my medication; I believe that my medications were never properly administered because of all his interference. It was also very difficult to know whether my symptoms were brought on by my husband or were symptomatic of BPD.

When we set out to divorce, he used my mental history to try to get full custody of the children. Against my therapists' approval, he had me hospitalized once again while he worked to get a restraining order against me. This time, my diagnosis was coupled with many inaccuracies that he gave the hospital, on intake, to try to make his case better. I knew there was no way that they had a proper evaluation of me, because he was telling them things that were untrue. So they changed my medications. I knew that I would not be able to rely on that regimen. The medications were very strong and had many side effects.

After being released, I decided that maybe my stability would come with detox from the meds. Now we were separated, and I was not going to be home with him or the children, so I would be able to use my DBT skills properly without him being able to stop me.

Despite the stress of divorce, finally being able to take care of myself, I was able to stabilize for the first time.

It has been four years since my son was born. About six years since the symptoms were the strongest. Two years of brutal custody evaluations, including multiple psychiatric evaluations done by child services and the court evaluator… and despite that stress and terror, I am holding steady.

It has been almost two years since I stopped taking medications and separated from my husband. Having the kids only 50 percent of the time gave me the time I needed to be able to dedicate healing time for myself. This would also be the first time he would not be intruding in my therapy; using DBT skills uninterrupted has given me the strength to overcome my symptoms.

My moods are more balanced. I no longer shop and buy things for comfort. I can also manage to buy only what I need and not buy in excess. I no longer check on the kids at night to see if they're breathing, and I sleep without sitting up hourly to listen for crying. I don't clean all day or fold the clothes perfectly and iron pillowcases. I don't feel the need to disclose all my private information to strangers. My promiscuous behavior and angry outbursts are under control. My obsessive, repetitive, and compulsive thoughts are at an all-time low. The paranoia is more like a bit of self-consciousness at this point.

I swim regularly and have changed the way I eat. I don't nap anymore, and I sleep straight through the night. I see my DBT therapist weekly and my psychiatrist about every quarter.

I believe that the pressures of being a wife and mother full-time, coupled with a controlling husband, held me back from recovery. I do believe that my illness contributed to much of the marital problems. Not that someone from a perfect childhood could've dealt better with the difficulties my BPD brought on the family, but my husband's own trauma made it difficult to follow the recommendations made by the therapists and doctors. Had he been a healthier and stronger person, not suffering from social anxiety and depression himself, maybe things would have been different. Perhaps he would not have felt the need to control me the way he did. And had I had a stronger support system and more positive reinforcement, maybe I would have been stronger, but that was not the situation. I had to battle my illness and deal with a difficult partner as well. I don't know whether things would have been that much different. BPD is an illness that can be trying even on a healthy family and spouse.

I still love him. He still loves me. Still, there was too much hurt on both sides to go back.

But I am moving forward, now thanks to DBT.

12. On the Other Side

Crossing the border is a precarious journey. It takes every-thing you have, challenges everything you believe, and com-pletely changes you. It is filled with moments of hopelessness and despair, and moments when you can see just enough light to believe that you can make it through. It is the most difficult journey you will ever take, but on the other side of the fence is a true freedom that is worth fighting for.

I was diagnosed with borderline personality disorder around 2011, at twenty years old. Throughout my life, I had always been competent, accomplished, and well put together, but suddenly, the pain that I carried could no longer stay hidden. I had spent the years prior to the diagnosis using alcohol, drugs, food, lack of food, and boys to avoid confront-ing the pain inside of me. And it worked. I prided myself on being completely broken on the inside but wearing my mask so well that no one would ever know. And even though the storm had been brewing for quite some time, I never thought it would actually erupt.

At eighteen, I had gotten into NYU, my dream school, and moved into an apartment on Washington Square Park with my boyfriend. I had finally gotten everything I wanted, but the depression was only getting worse. I tried to distract myself from the misery by going to trendy restaurants,

Broadway shows, and chic hangouts. But the darkness followed me everywhere I went. Eventually, going to class became too difficult. I had always been able to push through my emotions, to show up when I didn't want to, and to mask the pain, but I just couldn't find the strength anymore. I called my mom, and she came to New York and spoke with each one of my teachers, who generously agreed to allow me to finish school from home. All I remember was spending weeks in bed, doing absolutely nothing but reflecting in disbelief on how my life was falling apart. I spent the next two years going to various treatment centers, raw food institutes, acupuncturists, meditation centers, and therapists. I had gotten relatively sober but had no way to cope with the raging storm inside of me. I knew there was something wrong with me; I just didn't know what it was or how to fix it.

My depression and anxiety continued to grow. Although I took online college classes, I pretty much stopped functioning. I spent all my time alone or with my mom, desperately depressed and pretty hopeless. In 2011, I started to mention my suicidal ideation to my therapist at the time, and she lovingly suggested that I find someone with more experience in treating that level of depression. By the grace of God, and after extensive research, I found an adherent DBT therapist and began another go at therapy. I had sessions once a week and took part in a skills group. Talking about the pain and agony I lived with seemed to be making it worse. If I thought I had already fallen apart, I was wrong. After a few months of DBT, I *really* fell apart. I suddenly became acutely aware of my suffering. My mind was cluttered with self-critical, self-defeating, and negative thoughts at all moments of the day. There was no reprieve; there was nowhere to escape. There was no way to make the thoughts stop attacking me. The only time I had a break from them was in my one hour of therapy. I waited all week for that one hour, when my therapist met me in my own personal hell. For one hour a week, I was not wholly alone down there.

For at least a solid year into therapy, I woke up and went to sleep wanting to die every single day. The thoughts bombarded me before I even got to open my eyes in the morning, stayed with me throughout the entire day, and haunted my dreams at night. I isolated myself completely, rarely leaving the house. I had lost my boyfriend and all my friends, and the only person left was my mom. This was not good. I spent all day with my mom because she was terrified to leave me alone, and I was terrified to be alone. One moment I would be begging her to kill me, convinced it was the right thing for her to do, and the next I would be verbally attacking her, accusing her of making me sick and incapable. Neither of us could understand how I went from perfect, smart, accomplished me to depressed, suicidal, impossible me. Every word, facial movement, or hand gesture my mom made triggered me. As the saying goes, I was like a third-degree burn victim. The slightest poke sent me into unbearable pain. My life was a constant crisis. I would rage against my mom multiple times per day, screaming at the top of my lungs, telling her how it was all her fault. I would follow her around the house, stand outside her locked door, and hurl insults at her. I punched holes in the walls several times. When all this failed to relieve the pain, I would bang my head against the wall repeatedly or engage in other kinds of self-harm. And after it was all out of me, I would fall to the floor covered in guilt and shame. I would beg her to kill me, insisting that if she truly loved me, she would euthanize me. *That's what a good, caring, loving mom would do. A good mom would not let her daughter suffer like this.* I went to bed around six o'clock every night, and trust me, six o'clock never came soon enough. From the moment I got up, I would count down the hours till I could go back to sleep again, to find some escape from my life. This was my day, every day, for about a year. This was my living hell.

Even after a full year of DBT, I still struggled with suicidal ideation. The pain I experienced was so great, and I always felt like, eventually, even if I never had the guts to take my own life, I would just disintegrate into the earth. After all, I was already completely dead on the inside. All that remained was my flesh. My therapist actually made me fill out this survey every time I saw her, and there was a question about suicidal ideation. I found relief in the idea of not having to exist anymore, not having to be in this pain, and I believed I always *would*—I couldn't even imagine a life without the pain. But, as many months passed, there would be times when I no longer thought of dying all day. This was progress. I started to buy into the notion that the painful emotions were a result of my distorted thoughts. I started to pay more attention to my thoughts—what they sounded like, how loud they were, and how they made me feel. I had moderate success in using certain DBT skills: mainly distract, opposite to emotion, a (rather novice) rendition of DEAR MAN, and the use of physical sensations. I was not the most skillful, but skillful enough to stay alive. The fights with my mom were just slightly less frequent and intense, indicating that I was making slow progress.

My self-harm urges and behaviors were occurring less and less often. I would leave my house to go to an outdoor market, a movie, or a restaurant—with my mom, of course. And although things were no longer getting worse, I was chronically unsatisfied with my progress and felt wholly responsible for what was happening to me. Some days, I still forget that this whole thing is actually a disorder.

After two years, I found God and began developing my spirituality. I found the courage to get a job at a local bakery, and I reached out to some old friends. I was still shrouded in darkness, but the ten-hour bakery days gave me a chance to be out of my house and out of my mind. It was hard—I was still consumed with negative thoughts and feelings. But I was moving, hallelujah. The more stable I became, the more I was able to dive into my thought life, figure out what it sounded like, why it wasn't working, and how I could change it. Although I still lived in emotion mind the majority of the time, I understood more and more what the heck a wise mind was and what it might sound like. I developed an awesome relationship with my therapist, and when I couldn't find a wise, compassionate, loving voice, I would borrow hers. There was something inside of me that saw a glimmer of hope, and it wouldn't let me give up.

I was diligent in using the DBT skills I understood. I certainly didn't always use them effectively, but I never stopped trying. I got discouraged and wanted to give up several times a day, but there was something inside of me that said, "No! You are too close! Keep it moving!" Layer by layer, peel by peel, I started discovering all the thoughts and beliefs that kept me miserable. It *felt* impossible, but it wasn't. I soaked up as much wisdom as I could in each therapy session and then returned hopeful to survive another week and see how skillful I could be. As I came to understand my thoughts, and how they caused feelings and body sensations, there was a shift. At some point I realized that I could be in charge of my brain, that I could control where I put my attention. That by using DBT skills, I could get out of suffering and into the present moment, where there was usually nothing wrong. Even when everything was going wrong, and nothing was working, everything was perfectly fine. I spent a long time shifting from wise mind to emotion mind, going back and forth all day, every day. I was going deep inside myself, determined to examine all the beliefs that held me in suffering and blocked my freedom.

I am equally excited and shocked to tell you that today, along with sadness and worry, I experience episodes of joy and peace. I didn't think it was possible, but it is. I overcame borderline personality disorder. I crossed the border, climbed the fence, and stepped into a beautiful, exciting new life that I never thought possible. There are difficult days, there are times when I am vulnerable, and there are times when I lose sight of the dream. But no one can take my wise mind from me. No one can steal my peace. I am safe, and I am free.

13. Survivor

Looking for support throughout my disorder has been like attempting to look for solace in a valley of landmines: all the recovery information I come across is about how others can recover from my existence. Article after article claims that I have no chance at normalcy, whatever that may be. Forum after forum claims that my scarlet letter dooms me to a lifetime of playing the victim and eternal distress. For some reason, few can imagine a life in which I'm happy and functional.

It may sound like a cliché, but I grew up a sensitive child. Riddled with oddities and sprinkles of what I later came to call abuse, my upbringing was chaotic. In my childhood mind, broken flowerpots justified guilt-ridden crying spells, and getting an answer wrong on a fourth-grade math exam was reason enough to cyclically doubt the progression of my future. People's body language and tone of voice seemed to affect me more than others appeared to be affected. I had intense negative feelings in response to my perceptions of body language or voice tonality in others.

Close bonds were never formed between me and other children, and when I finally found myself dating, my relationships became even more erratic. Eventually I came to accept myself as the "crazy one," finding it easier to marginalize myself than to think about the fact that I might have to take responsibility for an illness. I hurt a lot of people, and it was easier to point the finger at them as triggers for my anger than to look at myself as the problem. It was easier for me to blame other people than to think about the fact that my oddities might have been more than mere oddities.

Throughout middle school, I formed friendships with other girls, but they were nothing more than shallow companionships to fill the pathology-riddled voids and nulls of my life. An aggressive and profound emptiness wove its way in and out, severing the relationships I attempted to form, time and time again. Quickly, I became used to the isolation. Watching others, it was almost as though they were all interconnected, while I sat on the sidelines brewing in my own angst and jealousy. Nobody could handle the chaos I brought to relationships, and seemingly nobody knew why that was.

My first episode was in Washington, DC, of all places, in a café. I was jealous that my two best friends had decided to have lunch with another friend of ours, and I felt such rage that I reacted by sleeping on the floor of our hotel room. There was no reason for such, but I told them that I didn't feel comfortable sleeping in the same bed as them. I got my period later that year.

In tenth grade, a companion of mine proudly displayed crimson lines carved into his arm, and curiosity got the best of me. He made it a point to flaunt his wounds to anybody who would look, and I figured it was something worth trying, as I'd heard of many people—much like drugs and alcohol—using it to cope. I went home that night and, out of cowardice, took a plastic knife to carve at my wrist. I kept cutting and cutting at my skin until I rubbed it raw. When I saw blood trickle down, I stopped. This tyranny only escalated into wrestling with my junior-year boyfriend for a baggie of pliable razor blades and falling asleep with blood-soaked towels my senior year. To the best of my knowledge, those blood-stained towels are still hiding in the cracks and crevices of my childhood room, along with many memories of depression, inadequacy, desperation, and abandonment.

My struggles with self-injury hit their peak my freshman and sophomore years of college, after a few particularly negative experiences with drinking and men. I sliced up both of my breasts with a razor blade, requiring stitches, as the nurses in the ER told me that I was far too beautiful to damage my precious skin. The psychiatrist on call told me—after going to the ER myself, knowing very well what had happened to me—that I wasn't assaulted due to the fact that I had consumed alcohol. At that point, things had reached their height. My moods were unmanageable, I was still self-injuring, college felt like too much, and I was so incredibly isolated due to my illness that simply getting by felt like a fantasy.

Then I met a very special young man. As soon as we met, everything seemingly went away. For a split second, I lost the ability to feel the tsunamis of emotion that seemed to rule my life, and I was simply able to be in the moment with him— gallivanting around town, getting frozen yogurt, cuddling in my dorm to watch *Criminal Minds* when I felt ill, and skipping class to screw in the most sensual of ways, when I didn't feel that invested in my schoolwork. I'd had relationships before, of course, but never had they really lasted more than a month or two. They usually started out with a surge of puppy love and lust, only to end with my dramatic flair and the most intense loathing. This was different, but still putting off the inevitable.

He stuck around, something I've never experienced before. I've become so accustomed to people being intolerant of my emotional reactions that I merely don't allow myself to get close to people anymore. It's much easier than getting close to people, and when I had episodes, he understood that my illness was a part of me but did not define me—an entity of sorts. He endured my unhealthy mood swings and tolerated the abuse I started to put forth. Everybody else in my life had left before I'd gotten to that stage of emotional distress, so I'd never known how to handle this sort of situation. He stuck around, not really knowing how to define true love, formulating a concept around unconditional terms and fantasies that were everlasting. He told me things were forever and that he would never leave. For somebody with such a black-and-white mind, that was both a blessing and a curse to hear.

I was physically abusive for the first—and hopefully the only—time in my life. It made me terrified of medication. Terrified of myself and the things I'm capable of, given any circumstances. I remember throwing my fists down onto cars, so hard that I had bruises the size of baseballs going down my arms. I was throwing sharp objects, shrilling at the top of my lungs, and running down the street after people at 3:00 a.m. in the absolute freezing cold in a bathrobe, just to continue screaming at them and abusing them. *I was an absolute horror.* I don't blame people for not wanting to be around me.

My experiences in the hospital were just horrifying beyond words—just more than I can fathom in the English language. I specifically recall incidents that stick out in my mind—ones that both horrify and devastate me. Incidents of a very ill schizophrenic woman speaking in graphic detail about the violent scenes playing behind her eyes always come to mind. I also remember, very much so, the loneliness and feelings of distrust I felt—for none of the doctors seemed to believe what I said while I was in there, yet they asked me, time and time again, what I was feeling and experiencing, while continuing to manipulate my medicine as I got progressively worse. A lot of the people surrounding me were not in touch with reality and would often act out in tantrums, making me feel rather isolated, questioning my sanity and safety. Daily, I looked forward to my two visitors toward the end of the day, but they often weren't able to make it—which devastated me. Being confined to that space, being treated as though I was not credible, and essentially being treated like a child, was unbearable. I don't ever want to go back to that again, and I'll do anything to avoid it. Eventually, to get out of the hospital, I ended up lying about my feelings, as the medicine changes never helped my situation, and being there made things ten times worse for me.

It will always be a fear of mine to return to being that person, or even a semblance of that person. My ex-boyfriend—somebody whom I loved very deeply and likely always will—has time and time again told me about nightmares he's had of me stabbing him and insane fears he has of me returning to that. It's so unfair that with any other illness, nobody holds your worst against you—only with mental illnesses is it held above your head, as though episodic mistakes and depressive actions are something you can control within the confines of relationships.

For three years, my illness persisted. He called it the normal ups and downs of love, while promising to change. I attempted to change our dynamic, attempting to change him as I turned a blind eye to the reality of our situation. I came to realize that he didn't love me and instead came to love the sick me—perhaps my illnesses—entirely too much. The puppy love had turned into codependency for him and a complete and utter isolation for me. We were both miserable, yet both too weak to end things out of desperation.

In group therapy one night, I was listening to a woman speak about her experiences with her alcoholic husband of fifteen years. Their relationship dynamic first horrified me, then deeply saddened me. It saddened me because I saw myself in her and her husband—my boyfriend and I at the time mirrored her and her husband perfectly. I didn't want to continue living a life of misery, and to be quite frank, I didn't see the point of living if I continued to lead such an existence.

I won't lie. When I go through periods where things become overwhelming, for a fleeting moment or two in the grand scheme of things, I do lose hope. However, if I truly did view things as despondent, I would have stopped existing quite a long time ago. With the range of emotions that I experience (being somebody with BPD), living takes a lot of work. It's not something I would commit to lightly.

I went home that night and ended things. Albeit not lightly—and quite impulsively—but it was for the best. The month or so following, I began to go through more than I'd gone through in my entire life. Throughout our relationship, I began working full-time on top of going to school full-time, so I was incredibly isolated; attempting to reach out to friends I'd lost touch with was hard. Crying spells dominated my time, and it took days upon days to lift my head enough to go to class. I ended up reaching out to my abusive parents—whom I hadn't communicated with for half a year or so—to depend upon again for financial and emotional support, for the time being. They didn't have my phone number until that point.

Things were hard, but I came to realize that I couldn't search for a simple solution for this disorder. Just as somebody with lung cancer can't search for a relationship to cover up the misery of their disease, I can't either. Being coddled and cuddled may help soothe the misery in the moment, but it doesn't dissolve things in actuality. If anything, it makes things worse to dismiss them as nonexistent when they are quite a large psychological elephant in the room. With BPD, relationships are complex, messy, and often riddled with projection as well as fear. They are not impossible but surely are challenging. For me, the relationship became a Band-Aid for a gaping wound.

For years, I went to school full-time. For years, I worked full-time. For years, I poured myself into the people I came across, without considering my mental health. For years, I reacted. Thinking about my actions wasn't feasible for me, and many of the therapists I saw didn't seem to take me seriously when I told them how much I was struggling. My ability to juggle work and school, as a workaholic, was somehow proof of their theory that I was more stable than I claimed, and that I was being dramatic in my claims of instability. The reality is that I'm merely good at putting on a smiling face. I suppressed my volatile emotions in favor of my compulsive need to please others, which fed into the perfectionism of being such a workaholic.

I felt as though things would never get better, but eventually they did. The crying spells lessened, and I reached out to friends, coming to find that I was a lot more supported and loved than I felt. Taking it as a time to work on my emotional struggles, I defined my emotional autonomy yet again, as opposed to giving into the suicidal thoughts that plagued my mind continually. I laid down my pride and took a break from working. I focused on my schoolwork and focused on my therapy—on my health.

I've come to find that my recovery is going to take time, and that while it may seem to be simple, it never will be easy. Those who stick around throughout the complex and messy process are those I truly consider to be friends. Often this disorder can be isolating, but never will I let it defeat me. The breakup at first was devastating for me, but I was able to turn it into something beautiful, for it showed me that relationships are meant to bring out the best in others and not to be built on dependence. From now on, I want to enter them out of interest and passion—not out of need and desperation.

This disorder is a living hell, but I know it's not impossible, which is what keeps me going, day by day. As J. D. Salinger once said, "I've survived a lot of things, and I'll probably survive this."

14. How to Build and Bust a Life

The year was 2008. As the country was devolving into racist, sexist, political preschoolers flinging poo and fighting over ownership of a rubber ducky, my own world was disintegrating and splintering into chaos. Death was a constant presence, its red eyes burning, as I lost one beloved cat and all four grand-parents to its cruel touch. One after the other, boom boom boom boom boom. Five deaths in five years, then one more, my eighteen-year-old orange tabby queen, Nessa, on December 3, 2012. The Mayan calendar's end date loomed, as if I needed reminding that life as I knew it was over.

I lost myself frequently in those days. I'd never heard of BPD and had no idea the extent of the havoc it was wracking in my mind. I was miserable, stuck in a dead-end job at the public library, watching people less qualified than me secure the promotion I kept trying to earn. The constant invalidation was infuriating and depressing. Eventually I stopped caring. In April 2008, after three years of wearing that face in the jar by the door, I finally left the library to pursue an internship at a small feminist publisher in Berkeley, California. I'd applied for an unpaid internship, but by the end of the interview, I had landed a paying job as a freelance proofreader. Getting my okay became the final step before a manuscript was approved and made into a book. I was beyond excited to finally have my foot in the door of the publishing industry, and I was good at my new job. My bosses soon realized my talent, and to my surprise and delight, they expanded my responsibilities and gave me a raise. After proofreading my second book, I discovered a community college program that offered certification in graphic design, emphasis on publishing. I enrolled, thrilled that finally I had a plan, perhaps even a life to build. I had hope. A future.

July 3, 2008. The day before my twenty-ninth birthday. I was sitting quietly at the DMV, waiting to renew my driver's license, when out of nowhere a terrible pain seared through my belly, leaving me gasping. My future flickered. The unknown pain was epicentered above my navel at my solar plexus, radiating muscle spasms, all accompanied by sky-high anxiety and a fatigue worthy of a weary Atlas. But I stupidly pushed through it all. Soon I began to have trouble with my proofreading. My head was filling with a dense fog that prevented me from translating ideas into words. Forget proper punctuation and reading comprehension. Splat and splat. The words swam and lost their meaning. I was drowning in exhaustion, but I still refused to give up. So my body did it for me. It was the third Monday of September, midway through typography class, when the abdominal pain hit with a new, horrible intensity. Scared I was about to vomit all over my school's computer lab, I sprinted to the ladies' room and tried to calm myself. I was inches from a full-blown panic attack. When breathing failed to calm, I popped an Ativan, grabbed my gear, and tried to get my teacher's attention. He ignored me. So I said, "Fuck it," and left. Walked out of that school and drove home, in pain, tears flowing, knowing that my last thread of hope for a future in publishing had just died. I sadly quit my job and dropped out of school. Very quietly, my dream was over.

I spent four miserable years trying to find the source of the pain. What was wrong with me? Why didn't my doctors seem the least bit concerned that I had this chronic, disabling abdominal pain, yet the numbers in all my tests, no matter how invasive, came back perfectly normal? All except the markers for inflammation; that was high. But despite the inflammatory proof that my body had indeed been compromised by pain, intense enough to activate those markers, my pleas for help and answers continued to fall on deaf ears. There was no version of DEAR MAN that was effective enough to get and keep my doctors' attention and focus. So I turned inward. Having survived a childhood of trauma, I figured I'd been in chronic fight-or-flight for years, possibly my whole life, and that accumulation of stress must've finally broken my body. Western doctors call it fibromyalgia. It was the only response resembling reality, and it felt like death. The hospital offered no real answers, only drugs I didn't want and violent violations of my body, especially in the ER. This was the very antithesis of healing. After four fruitless years, my GI doctor, almost as a last resort, suggested we try the fibromyalgia pressure-point diagnostic test. I reacted to seventeen of the eighteen trigger points. Mystery solved. But the BPD remained undiagnosed, and my mind soon began to spin wildly out of control.

I finally had my diagnosis, but it was another four years of trial and error, with medications, herbs, and supplements, before I finally had the pain managed at a tolerable level. After the first several months of being trapped in a chair in distress tolerance, pain management mode, I began to feel and relate to life on a deeper level. The more life I lost, the more I appreciated the perfect, vivid beauty of a rose, or a redwood, or sunlight reflecting off the bay. I felt every tiny spasm from my digestive, intestinal, and reproductive systems, so I was in pain pretty much constantly. My overloaded brain sparked and popped, short-circuiting wise mind, and soon I began to break down. Raw and wounded, I felt everything. The earth's electromagnetic field connecting to each of my cells. The climate changing. The energy emanating from rocks and crystals, ley lines and fault lines, even the seismic waves from Japan's 9-pointer in 2011. It was as though my brain had adapted to my forcibly lost mobility by expanding its capacity to sense unseen energy. Call it a sixth sense, or the Cassandra complex, or unsimple logic. But I could see clearly what others couldn't, especially the inevitabilities that would occur, should events continue on their paths unchanged. Then, in December 2012, something that awes me still…the shockingly clear cat-whispering session, aided by a pendulum, that I had with my dying orange tabby alpha queen, Nessa. That was the night she took her last breath, in my arms, her head resting on my heart. I still get teary, thinking about it. Her death was a tipping point. The grief overwhelmed and consumed me. I was despondent, spending most of my time crying, doubled over in pain, and fighting with family, not understanding why my brain kept shooting sparks and bouncing between extremes, knowing only that something was very wrong and still very unexplained. It was late 2013 when I finally found out about BPD and DBT.

My brain, I learned, is...quirky. It doesn't process pain right. Physical pain, emotional pain, my brain just goes FZZZZT until I fear for my sanity. Western doctors call this borderline personality disorder, perhaps one of the worst, most ugly misnomers in the medical world. Sounds dangerous, deranged. It's not. But it is a thing, an actual thing. I wasn't crazy. I wasn't losing my grasp on reality. I had BPD, and my poor foggy brain was simply overwhelmed by everything I was sensing, to the point of complete nervous breakdown. DBT classes began in 2014, and very slowly but surely, I learned how to turn my mind toward how harshly I view and judge myself and how I deal with the world. But it's a constant daily strug-gle just to maintain my equilibrium. I've lost nearly eight years of life—prime years, ages twenty-eight to thirty-five—and I will never get it back. Radically accepting that lost life isn't easy, probably because it's still happening to this day.

Back in 2009, the pain was bad enough to keep me home-bound and, on some days, chair-bound. I discovered quickly how debilitating, exhausting, and deeply depressing it was, living with chronic pain. Longing for life, I found solace in music and found that going to rock concerts made me feel alive, truly alive to my very core. My love for music and excite-ment at seeing my favorite bands live dulled the pain just enough so that I could do it. Having a concert on the calendar meant that for at least one night I would feel fully alive. It was my way of clinging to hope, to life, of accumulating positives and taking opposite action, and fighting my damnedest to not slide down that spiral to a fiery, hellish underworld. And for the majority of events, it worked.

But there were times. There *are* times. Living with chronic pain, like BPD, takes severe patience, discipline, and self-knowledge. It is absolutely exhausting on every level to have to be so constantly aware, to have to keep employing DBT skills over and over and over again, only to watch those skills break apart under pressure. There is no warning when something's about to go south, and things can go south so fast. Body and mind, either or both. Eight years behind on life, yet no matter what I do to catch up, it seems I'm always, always late. How can I ever catch up on life if I'm always late in the now? I can't. How will I heal if I miss half my therapy? I won't!

My calendars tell the story, with years of blacked-out dates to missed appointments, rock concerts, musicals and theater, and Oakland A's baseball games...the only things that got my blood pumping and made me feel alive. But because I'm hurting and moving so damn slowly now, it's far too easy to become really, really late. And the minutes count—oh, do they ever. Six minutes late to John Leguizamo's *Klass Klown* at Berkeley Rep, and I'm banished to a hallway with a small, grainy TV. That show later went to Broadway as *Ghetto Klown*. Eight minutes late for *Wicked* at the Orpheum in San Francisco, and I have to wait twenty-two minutes before I'm allowed to my seat. Twenty seconds late to BART (Bay Area Rapid Transit)? That instantly becomes twenty minutes late to *American Idiot*, *Passing Strange*, and *Avenue Q*. I was an hour and a half late to Green Day's last show at the Greek Theatre and missed several concerts altogether—Paramore, New Found Glory, Tegan and Sara, Metric, AFI, Thirty Seconds to Mars, Pearl Jam, Soundgarden, Bridge School Benefit, Live 105's BFD and Not So Silent Night...and so many baseball games on both sides of the bay. So much money, so carefully saved and spent, lost. Life experiences, gone forever.

Then there are the days when I'm actively flaring, both body and mind a swirling foggy mix of pain and desperation, until I end up curled in a ball on the floor, crying, and I fear this is it, this is my life, my legacy—my legacy is losing life. Time is the only true measurement of existence. If I'm late or can't go, losing my time to pain, meds, and oblivion…if my seat remains empty, do I still exist?

Learning DBT was like finding the Rosetta stone to my foggy fibro, BPD brain. Suddenly I understood. Everything became so clear. Building skills like mindfulness, distress tolerance, emotional regulation, and interpersonal effectiveness has drastically changed how I see, interpret, and respond to the world, as well as to myself. I'm handling crises better. I no longer have a complete mental breakdown when I'm late or losing life, which is huge for me. I'm trying very hard to remain mindful, being more fluid and open to going with the flow. Trouble is, despite everything, I'm still late, so I'm still losing life, and money, and respect, and self-worth. I don't know how to fix this. Wise mind, checking facts, problem solving, coping ahead, radical acceptance—none of these have thus far worked in rebuilding mastery of my time and, consequently, my life. I've mindfully made the decision that when the hospital or pharmacy screws me over, I am to act confused, *not* angry. They wouldn't hear me or help me if I did; they tune out angry. I'll never get what I need if I turn into Hulk Smash, even though smashing is often exactly what's needed. But it's also a very ineffective way to get what you want. Instead of anger, I choose to project confusion, giving them the chance to do their jobs competently. But being late all the time? How do you DEAR MAN soul exhaustion? How do you not go bust when every choice is busted? I don't know. Yet.

Life is a paradox. It is so random and fragile; a thin layer of skin is all that's protecting the precious blood in our veins. I can see and trace that pumping proof of life in my wrists, feel it thumping in my throat. When all hope seems lost, I cling to that proof. My heart is beating. I am alive. I could curl into a fetal position and cry for days, unable to deal with the audacities of my own brain, and before DBT, that was often my miserable reality. But deep down inside, lurking in the shadows of ancestral memory, my Athena self still lives, as does the stubborn refusal to let my demons win. I've been built, busted, rebuilt, busted again, and I'm still here. I am the moss that grows between bricks, the single California poppy standing tall after the earth has been ransacked and paved, the ancient oak tree whose roots have uplifted the sidewalk. Somehow, life finds a way.

15. I Am a Scientist

Feelings. Ever since I can remember, I knew there was something different about me because of my feelings. I was super sensitive, took everything literally, and was reactive. Then, to add to the complication, I began to engage in self-harm as an adolescent, usually as a result of fights with my father. We never agreed and still don't. About the only safe thing we can talk about is baseball. I moved out of the house as soon as I could after high school and worked a couple jobs before applying to UC San Diego. I stopped engaging in self-harm during this time and excelled in school. So much so, I applied to graduate school in the neurosciences and was happily accepted. But my emotions began to unravel with the pressures of getting a PhD. As the stressors of getting a degree increased, so did my emotions, and I found myself on an emotional roller coaster, which led to my first hospitalization, one week before my oral examinations. I have been hospitalized many times in my lifetime, and I have never found hospitals to be particularly stabilizing environments. Just a place to bide your time until your time is up. I left the mental hospital on, I think, a Wednesday, and took my oral qualifying examinations the next morning. Thankfully, I passed. Triumph over my emotions. I was unmedicated at this point. Unable to say no to added responsibilities, I took on duties beyond my dissertation, thus increasing my stressors to finish my PhD. I just couldn't say no to helping everyone except myself. My self-esteem was at an all-time low as I watched my fellow students complete their degrees and move forward with their careers. Additionally, I found myself watching my marriage fail before my eyes. It was all too intense, and I began my first experience with cutting. All I can tell you is that I was experiencing the most intense emotional pain at that moment, and for some reason, it came completely naturally to me to pick up a steak knife and cut to temporarily reduce the suffering. I carved a cross, as my father is a minister. I never feel a thing when I cut. Never. I see the sharp object going into my skin, and I wait for signs of harm. And then I feel relief on a lot of levels. This was another setback in my psychological health, as I hadn't self-harmed since I was a teenager. So now, I felt like a mutant for cutting; I had a divorce looming and a PhD to finish. Well, I divorced and moved into my own place. Brought home two cats and a dog that bites. I rescued them from shelters. And thought to myself it would be a good time to volunteer, right in the midst of the most pressure to finish my degree. Again taking on too much. I was then hospitalized a second time in graduate school. But I was determined to finish. And I had a mentor who was encouraging. I had a lot of friends at this point. I've never found it hard to make friends, and I tend to get along really well with others. Oftentimes, my mentors have told me that "everyone likes you here." It's in part because I am a people pleaser. I want others to be happy, even at my own expense. But my friendships were never enough to sustain the emotions that I felt and how I felt about myself. But I passed. Despite my hospitalizations and unstable emotions, I finished my PhD in the neurosciences. I wrote my thesis and gave my oral defense in front of a large crowd of people. One of my mentors said it was the most people he had ever seen at a defense, and he was eighty years old. Honestly, it was a breeze. Easier than writing my thesis, and the chair of my committee told everyone it was the best defense that he had ever seen. I've never been so stressed as when I divorced and finished my PhD. But I soon landed a job at a prestigious university and was on my way to becoming a neuroscientist. To add to being borderline, I found that I was comorbid for psychosis and found myself paranoid. I was cutting, burning pictures of myself, and frankly creating so much art. But because of my paranoia, I decided to leave the university, as I thought my colleagues and mentor were out to get me. Very sad. And true to borderline, I packed up my belongings and drove across the country, on a whim, and landed in Washington, DC, near Howard University. I had a job interview lined up. Miraculously. But I was functioning at such a low level that I couldn't find my way to my interview. I made an appointment with a psychiatrist but could never make it there. And so I decided to move back to California. I had to find a job fast and applied for a teaching position at a university and was hired the same day I applied. Luck. This was a period of medication. Antipsychotics. I held the job for three years and took a job at a university in Los Angeles, for research. I met a lifelong friend and colleague while at a hospital in LA. She has been a tremendous support. It was a stressful time, working two academic jobs, and I'm not quite sure how I managed it without cutting. But I didn't. I fell into an inappropriate relationship while at the university that proved to be chaotic, fraught with intense emotion, and he couldn't handle my extravagant spending. I gave away so much money to charities and friends, until it was all gone and I had nothing left to give. My job at the university in Los Angeles was coming to an end, and I wanted to stay in research rather than teaching, so I applied to research jobs. To my amazement, a prestigious Ivy League university was interested in me and flew me out for an interview—which I aced, even though I was psychotic—and was offered the job. I was ecstatic. It was awesome. Dream job. One problem, though. When I started, I was acutely aware of everything I could use to cut. Nonstop. If I saw paper, I thought *paper cut*. If I cut lemons for the experiment with a knife, I thought, *Cut myself*. It was incessant. I think it lasted for a full month. But I didn't cut that whole time. It was a struggle of the mind. I don't remember being particularly stressed. I always felt at ease at the university. And the experiments weren't stressful. I didn't know a single person in the university town when I moved, but I made friends fast both at the lab and at a local coffee shop. I became close with a philosophy professor and a computer science professor in their sixties who took me home for Thanksgiving and introduced me to their sons. I kept my emotions at bay. Saw a psychiatrist for therapy and medication and saw my psychotherapist of almost twenty years via Skype. She cured me of my PTSD. She is amazing. But my appointment at the university was only for two years, and as the ending approached, I was experiencing intense mood swings and emotional instability with the stress of finding a job. I had several interviews, but none panned out. My best friend, who is also a tremendous support, said he would fly me and my dog back to California and I could live with him. I was very emotionally unstable. Severed most of my friendships from the university. Cried all day and night and was unmedicated. Big mistake. I heard voices all day long and every day, telling me someone was being abused. It was excruciatingly painful. This is where I decided I couldn't stand the emotional pain one day longer, and my borderline brain kicked in to self-harm. I swallowed every pill I could get my hands on and chased it down with whiskey. My best friend found me the next day, unconscious, and called the paramedics. I think I woke up five days later in a hospital in Santa Monica. My suicide plan had not worked. And I was headed back to a mental institution that was of no use. Clearly, I needed to get back on meds and in therapy. But a caveat: I didn't like my psychiatrist. She informed me that I would never ever work again and the sooner I get could used to that idea, the better it would be. My caseworker felt differently. But to spite my psychiatrist, I stopped my medications. It was a case of opposing viewpoints, because my caseworker felt I should join Mensa, take yoga at an art museum, and start looking for jobs. But the psychiatrist's words stuck in my head, and I felt distraught. This was another turning point, where I decided to abruptly pack up my things, hitch a ride from a stranger on Craigslist, and head north of Los Angeles, without a plan. I thought I'd find an apartment in three days. There was no logic. There was no apartment. I found myself without money and homeless with a yoga mat, all kinds of emotions going through my head, not to mention I was hearing voices. I think one month later, a very kind forest ranger rescued me with a sandwich and a drink, and I went into a mental institution yet again. I did not want to be medicated. I thought I was fine. There was no logic. They let me out fifteen days later. I stayed with the forest ranger and his wife until they said I needed to stay at the shelter. I decided to take off up north and started hitchhiking and walking until I made it to Chico. Men picking me up along the way asking for blow jobs. I was indignant. Told them to stop the truck. One man said he was going to a park. I screamed as loud as I could, "Stop." I got out of a moving car and I wrote the license plate down. I called the cops, gave them the number, and they were nonplussed. Nothing we can do in this situation, even though the man was offering a very borderline and psychotic ill woman a ride in exchange for a blow job, once he already had me in the car. There is no justice. I walked my way to a state university, where I felt for certain I would find help. Instead, I was put in handcuffs, taken to a police station, and kept in handcuffs and taken to a hospital. I escaped my room to try to find a shower, because I hadn't had a shower in days, but was caught in the shower. From there, I was back in a mental institution for two weeks. I talked to my best friend and my cousin, who said my brother would be there to pick me up. And when I came home with my brother, I started therapy and saw a psychiatrist who diagnosed me with bipolar disorder and psychosis. Later, I was diagnosed with borderline, because I started cutting again and had the characteristic features of borderline. And even later, I was diagnosed with OCD. I think that makes four disorders in total. But this is a story of borderline. So I will say that I have been in dialectical behavior therapy for one year. Group and individual therapy. I have not cut for one year. It is still a struggle sometimes not to self-harm. I have problems with my romantic relationships, where if people do not get back to me right away, I feel a swarm of emotional pain and unjustified shame. I fixate on the relationships and almost always want to end them that same day. There is no way that they can be too busy to get back to me and care about me. I am unable to hold the dialectic in my mind. And no one can convince me that they still care about me. It happens to me almost every day. And if they do get back to me, I feel happy for the rest of the day, but the next morning, the memory of the happy feeling is gone, and I start all over again. The happy feeling lasts but for hours. It is never continuous. But I have a bevy of DBT skills to rely upon, not to mention skills coaching from some pretty awesome therapists. I just applied to almost twenty jobs. I am hopeful that I will one day return to research, have a healthy relationship, and find my own apartment again. I am a dedicated person, so no matter how long it takes, I will achieve these goals. Despite my feelings.

16. There Is a Yolk Under Those Shells

We all know there is stigma around all mental illnesses, but the stigma around people with BPD is off the charts. Below are a few examples:

- You feel like you are walking on eggshells around them.

- They are miserable people who just want to make everyone around them miserable.

- They cause trauma and pain in their loved ones' lives.

- They stalk their partners if they try to leave.

- They physically and verbally attack others for no reason.

- They blame everyone else for their problems.

- They threaten suicide or to hurt themselves, for attention or to manipulate others to do something for them.

- They are the worst patients, noncompliant and draining.

- They don't want help, don't try, are lazy, over-react to everything, are too sensitive, don't care about anyone but themselves, don't feel guilt for hurting their loved ones.

- In the movies and TV: they boil rabbits, kill animals, stalk their partners, and kill anyone who gets in their way.

- There are two kinds of BPs: the high-functioning (blaming) BPs (aka the "invisible" BPs), who don't think there is anything wrong with them and won't get treatment; and the low-functioning BPs, or "consumers" because they "consume" mental health services. In other words, they are treatment seeking.

Sorry, I can't help myself; I have to address this one. Talk about black-and-white thinking! We are either this or that. While I find this kind of ironic (comments like this also amuse me, when "normal" people exhibit one of *our* symptoms, but that's just my sense of humor), I really find it sad. It seems to me, by putting us into one of those two boxes, we're damned if we seek treatment and we're damned if we don't. Either way, we suck! At least that's how I took it when I first read it. I also disagree that the high-functioning (blaming) BPs are the "invisible" BPs. We all know they exist, including the professionals; we read about them all the time. They are the ones who just haven't sought treatment yet.

Personally, I think the real invisible BPs are those who have sought treatment, learned the skills to manage their illness, and enjoy less chaotic lives. We are the invisible BPs, because with the stigma surrounding this disorder, some of us can't afford to out ourselves. So we hide, we remain anonymous, so many people don't think we exist. A few brave souls have come out, and I applaud them. I wish I could be that brave—maybe someday.

The list of stigma goes on, but you get the idea. These are just some of the things I read and hear about myself every day. And though I know I have caused pain and chaos in my loved ones' lives, blamed others for my problems, had angry outbursts, justified my actions, been noncompliant, been overly sensitive, verbally attacked others, threatened to commit suicide, attempted suicide several times, had self-destructive behaviors, tested my boyfriends, therapists, and others to see if they'd stay, ended relationships before others could leave me, gotten into physical fights at school and with my siblings, changed majors and jobs often, I didn't know why. All I knew was that I was hurt, angry, frustrated, hopeless, and exhausted. The only way I knew how to deal with it was to lash out at others or hurt myself, which, in turn, made other people hurt, angry, frustrated, hopeless, and exhausted. It was a mess.

Yes, I did do all those things, but here's what you may not know. While I may have made my loved ones' lives miserable, I *definitely did not* wake up in the morning and ask myself how I could make everyone's life miserable today. I *did* feel bad when I hurt them. I *did* (and still do) feel like a horrible person. I may not have shown it. I put on my badass front, said all those mean things, stormed out, left them feeling as if I was right and they were wrong. Then, I went into my room or out the door, and I cried. I *did* know something was wrong with me. I just didn't agree with what they said it was, so I certainly wasn't going to admit it. I wanted to be good, I did try, and I just kept failing. Every day, I begged God to help me stop being that awful person, that baby, a bitch. I asked him to make *me* stop, make *them* stop, or at least help them understand me. When none of that was happening, that's when I hurt myself or became suicidal. In my mind, it was the only solution to end the pain—not just mine but theirs too.

Even with all my behaviors, the chaos I caused, and making my family feel like they had to walk on eggshells, we all knew there was another side to me, the *yolk*. I am smart, and have a great sense of humor; I got good grades in school, had friends, was good at sports, had boyfriends, and later had a wonderful fiancé. After graduating from college, I had great jobs; I always had a home, a car, and animals that I loved; I enjoyed reading, the theater, music, amusement parks, and traveling. No one (including me) understood why I was so miserable when I had all those things.

After getting help, my family and I now understand that we were *all* playing the blame game. When I said something that someone had said or done hurt or angered me, I was told that I was too sensitive, I was overreacting, I'd misinterpreted what they'd said, I should stop being such a baby, I should suck it up. "Life's not fair." "Why are you crying? It's not that big of a deal." And I always loved this one: "It wasn't my intention." To me, "It wasn't my intention" is not an apology, nor is it an acknowledgment that what they said or did hurt me; instead, it is a defense. That it was not their intention (and I totally get that this was true) negated the fact that what happened, or was said, still hurt or affected me in some way. So, therefore, since it wasn't their intention, or I had misinterpreted what they said or did, my feelings or reactions were unjustified—so, I was wrong, bad, or crazy. This is what caused the chaos: because I didn't have "normal" reactions to things, they blamed me; and because they didn't understand or validate my feelings or reactions, I blamed them. I told them that if they would only do this or stop doing that, then my life would be better, and they said the same thing back to me. It was an endless battle, and no one was winning.

We know better now. It wasn't *anyone's* fault. We were both right, and we were both wrong. There was something wrong with me; I had an illness, and we just didn't understand it or know how to deal with it. When a family member has an illness, be it mental or physical, it affects everyone around them. Therefore, *everyone* needs help to deal with it, not just the person with the illness. Thankfully, my loved ones did support me. They came to friends and family sessions that my DBT program offered to help educate family members about BPD and DBT. My sister went to the Family Connections program offered by the National Education Alliance for Borderline Personality Disorder and learned the skills for family members dealing with a loved one with BPD. Our relationships are better than ever.

Recovery

Even though there were signs in my younger years—suggestions from grammar school that we go to family therapy; an attempted suicide at seventeen, landing me in the ER, where they stitched me up and let me go without notifying my parent or suggesting any follow-up—I did not begin therapy until my early thirties.

I was having issues with stress, depression, and anxiety. There were going to be several layoffs in my company. Since I was the payroll coordinator, I was in on what was happening and who was going to be laid off. And, as did all the other managers, I had to decide who would be laid off in my own department. These people were not just our coworkers but our friends, people we had gotten to know and care about. I was going to have to serve them this blow, which is a big loss to have to experience. My boss saw what a difficult time I was having and suggested I go see her therapist, and I did. For this, I will always be grateful to her. She directed me to one of the most important persons in my life.

At first, we just talked about what was going on at work and how unfair and awful I thought it was. We talked about my family and my history, at least the parts I was willing to share. I had major trust issues, so I wasn't about to tell all, at least not yet. He saw the person who complained about her loved ones, bosses, coworkers, friends, and society in general, the one who wanted everyone else to change so that her life would be better. Because I didn't like people to see me be vulnerable, I would often tell my stories using humor and sarcasm, so he got to see the funny side of me. Looking back, I think this was a good decision, because while he listened and heard, laughed with me, agreed or disagreed with me, he put me on my journey to trust and recovery. He knew that under that complaining, humor, sarcasm, and tough persona, there was a very sensitive, compassionate human being—he saw the *yolk*.

We continued to work together on my family issues, work issues, and anything else that life handed me. After a while, I let my guard down. I started to tell him about the things I never told anyone, all the things that had happened to me, that I was sexually abused by my grandfather and an older boy in my neighborhood, how I had become promiscuous, gotten pregnant and had an abortion, been mean to my loved ones. I told him about the shame I was carrying, the guilt I felt about all those things. I told him I was an awful person, and if people really knew all those things, they would hate me. I hated myself, and I just wanted to die.

After a suicide attempt, I was always sent to dual-diagnosis programs, because I had used alcohol and my meds to overdose. They told me these programs would help me with my problems, but I still wasn't getting better. I tried to explain to them that I did not have an addiction problem, I had a suicide problem; pills and alcohol was just a tool. No one at those programs would listen to me! The only one who got that part was my therapist, because he knew me and my lifestyle. The thing they all agreed on was I suffered from depression.

During one of my hospitalizations, rather than verbally trying to explain this *again*, I wrote a letter to the therapist who was treating me, and in the letter, I asked her, "If I hooked up a hose to my exhaust, would you send me to treatment for exhaust abuse? If you really want to help me, help me figure out *why* I want to kill myself, instead of treating me for how I choose to do it." After she showed my letter to the psychiatrist there, he talked with my therapist and listened to him when he said it wasn't substances; they saw that I met the criteria and was suffering from BPD. Wow! If only I had thought of that analogy sooner!

Now I knew what was wrong, it had a name, there was a treatment for it called DBT, and I wasn't the only one who had it. Even though it came with all the stigma I talked about, I didn't care, because now I had hope—*maybe I can get better.* So, that's what my therapist and I did; we found a wonderful DBT program, and I started on my road to recovery from BPD.

DBT has taught me the skills I needed to help manage my illness. I deal much better with stressful life events. I am able to stop and think before acting on impulses. I have effective coping skills to replace the self-destructive ones I was using. I still have moments or lapses; I'm just better able to get back to baseline or back on my recovery process quicker.

I still struggle with the fact that I have to hide a part of myself, mostly due to the stigma, which feeds the fears of abandonment. I go through life wondering: *What would happen if they found out? Would they still like me? Would they be afraid of me? Would they let me teach or be around their children?* While I know my illness doesn't define me, just as my job doesn't, it *is* a part of who I am. How can I have a true identity when I always have to keep my guard up and perform so that no one finds out? I don't feel that everyone has to know, but I would like the people close to me to know, so that I would have the answers to those questions my mind shoots at me.

As far as the emptiness issue goes, I have no idea about how this one gets fixed. As I have said, I have a great family, I do have friends, I love my job (it is very rewarding), I socialize, and I enjoy many activities, so it's not the lack of those things. Maybe when the stigma is gone, and I am no longer reminded of the monster I was, I can truly forgive and love myself, or maybe when I no longer have to perform or hide—and I know that people truly love and accept all of me—that emptiness will be filled.

I want to end with my gratitude. I am so grateful to all the professionals who do everything they can to help people suffering from BPD and their families deal with this illness, who educate others to try to decrease the stigma, and who have personally helped me along the way. I am most grateful to my therapist, who hung in with me no matter what I threw at him, helped and supported me in every way he could, and helped me find the DBT treatment I so desperately needed. He led me to another very important person, the head of the DBT program I attended, who also saw the *yolk* and never gave up on me. I am grateful and blessed to have had both of them in my life and on my journey toward recovery.

17. My Destructive Patterns Characterizing My Borderline Personality

I am twenty-nine years of age. I was diagnosed with borderline personality disorder in January 2010, during my first hospitalization, after attempting suicide. Although it was my first time being committed in a hospital, it was not my first attempt at suicide.

I was only a child when I would fantasize suicide. I would gaze in the mirror for an extended period of time saying things to myself like "You're so ugly" and "No one likes you." I knew it wasn't normal to think about dying all the time. I just wanted to be normal. It was around that time in my life, upon turning twelve, that I would discover alcohol. I began binge drinking to the point of blacking out. This pattern of coping became an ongoing cycle that I still struggle with to this day.

Life at home was terrorizing, to say the least. Verbal, emotional, and physical abuse, severe neglect in all aspects. I again would fantasize about growing up and awaiting someone to rescue me from my nightmare. Which became another pattern in my future relationships. My never-ending search for "the one." Who would save me? Who would take care of me?

I felt unloved, abandoned, rejected, and never good enough. A maternal narcissistic relationship with my mother, who used the face of psychosomatic illnesses to have me care for her needs. My needs were never met. This programmed me well to base my relationships on what I could do for others as my way to earn love, setting the stage for another pattern.

My oldest brother was the only one who I felt loved me. He was a heroin addict. Life consisted of writing letters to him in prison and visiting him in these institutions. I would often write him poetry and threaten him with suicide if he didn't comply with my demands to quit using drugs. A codependent relationship of "choose me over your drugs" began at a young age and still has been my pattern in these codependent/dependent relationships. Depending on whom I am with, I can bounce back and forth between these roles, hoping to have those buried childhood needs met and to ultimately be loved.

Although I would be in relationships, I would still feel this gaping hole deep within, and my destructive behavior would result in my efforts to avoid feeling or being alone with myself. I say "relationships" because I could never have just one commitment to someone. I would have multiple back doors open, as well as the "just in case" person if one of these fell through. My pattern to avoid the pain of abandonment. Really, by doing this I robbed myself of ever having a healthy commitment.

When I would start to feel this gaping hole, as I mentioned previously, it would feel as if my skin were crawling, as if my insides were trying to escape outside. I would frantically pace back and forth in the room, pull my hair, dig my nails into my skin, until finally fleeing the house only to disappear into the bottle again. There was no stopping in the moment at times like these. It wasn't until I took the dialectical behavior therapy program that, in time, I learned what self-awareness was and recognized these patterns.

I learned how to stop myself somewhere in the middle amongst my all-or-nothing thinking. My typical thought process would sound something like this: "Well, so-and-so doesn't want to be my friend, so I might as well die." Whenever I felt I was losing someone, or they didn't want me, is when it would hurt the most and when I would attempt suicide. I valued myself on the basis of other people's opinions of me. I could not communicate any difficult emotions I had; instead, I would self-harm or do reckless behavior in order to show someone how they were making me feel or to manipulate them into not leaving me. I recall saying, after one breakup, "I cut my arm, and he still doesn't want to be with me." I was completely adrift for lack of an identity. I would be whoever you wanted me to be, further losing myself in this process. I still am working on finding out who I am. In therapy, my doctor would stop me from speaking for a moment and say, "I don't want to hear what your friends want. What do *you* want?" My response was, "I don't understand the question." I'd never thought about what *I* wanted before. What if what I wanted caused someone to not like me and reject me? I could not handle that. I was self-doubting and indecisive, for fear my decision would upset someone. This was my pattern of people pleasing.

When I am in an environment that is uncertain, unpredictable, or just right out of control, I have severe anxiety and physical symptoms that accompany that. Internally, I suffer chronic pain, tense muscles, and upset stomach—indigestion, ulcers, to name a few. Outwardly, I try to control the environment around me, by being controlling, rigid, and a perfectionist. I am also overly jealous and suspicious in relationships. I am aware now that I have an anxious attachment system, so I am learning to be more cognitively balanced. I am still that little girl who craves a nurturing mother, but I am learning to parent myself now and learning to have adult relationships.

My growth and challenges in therapy have been learning boundaries and assertiveness. Recognizing my limitations, to say no when I need to. Trusting myself, my intuition, and listening to that inner voice. Spending time alone with myself and practicing different self-soothing and distress-tolerance skills instead of going on autopilot with destructive coping patterns. Radical acceptance still proves to be a challenge for me today. The emotional roller coaster is relentless, exhausting, and many times intolerable. I am left confused and terrified. I remember feeling that I was better off locked up in a cage than out in the world on my own. I would try to force myself into the hospital, begging to be admitted in order to be cared for, to be protected. It was a nest, a security, a home.

Living with BPD is a battlefield. I am learning about my triggers and how to avoid them, yet there are still many triggers that at times I didn't know were even there. Every now and again, I'll step on one of these landmines, or triggers, and am hit with my own self-destruction, but it is a battle I am not willing to lose, because *it means my life.*

18. Walking

Eggshells. That word makes me wince. It's like my N-word. It hurts to hear it, so I try not to use it. Even within the boundaries of its literal definition, I abandon the two-syllabled plural noun in favor of roundabout circumlocutions. Like a child with a speech impediment who shies away from difficult words, I speak of the exteriors of the ova, the shells of the egg, the eggs' shells, and so on.

When eggshells are employed figuratively, such as with the book *Stop Walking on Eggshells: Taking Your Life Back When Someone You Care About Has Borderline Personality Disorder*, my aversion spirals into apoplexy. It's not simply the idiom itself or, by extension, the bemoaning of an interpersonal relationship with redundant analogies to cracked eggs. No. The antipathy to all of it began with the guys that I dated.

One by one, in active succession, I was sideswiped with "I feel like I'm walking on eggshells" by each boyfriend, right around the time they became an ex-boyfriend. So accustomed am I to hearing the term referenced within that framework that I now associate the word "eggshells" with failed relationships, entirely. Think of Pavlov and his dogs. I'm the dog, that word "eggshells" is the bell, and instead of food, someone is getting broken up with. Usually me.

I'm a bit smarter than a dog, though. I like to think so. And intellectually I know that one small word does not carry the voodoo necessary to make a loving relationship fall to the wayside in the way that innocent lambs fall in slaughterhouses. Nor is there a little brat of a fairy fluttering about, whispering those nine otherwise insignificant conjoined letters into my significant others' ears, then leaving that annoying aforementioned book underneath their pillows at night.

No, I have a knack for creating that kind of magic all on my own. It's a gift, in the way that time bombs and improvised explosive devices are gifts. The eggshells are already there, rattling around in my brain, and at the end of every relationship, there I am, picking up the pieces.

It's not just romantic couplings, either. It's roommates, too. And friends. And coworkers. And family. The latter examples rarely use the word "eggshells," but they will similarly delete my number, cut me off, ignore my apologies, and discontinue association.

My first summer in college, I woke up in an ER with alcohol poisoning. "You almost died," my grandmother said to me several days later, over the phone. What she said probably should have meant more to me, but what I remember most is the way that she said it. Resignation without judgment, defeat. It crushed me. But not so much that I wasn't able to spit out an incendiary "Fuck you," right before she hung up on me.

The next time I heard anything from or about my grandmother, it was a cold February day three years later. I was twenty-two; she was waxy and stiff inside a coffin.

Guilt is easier to forgive than it is to forget. I haven't just done this once; there was another now deceased relative, a different story with the same ending. And another one after that. I told my eighty-two-year-old father, "I'm going to let you rot. I'm going to let you die." I can forgive myself for being childish and stupid, but I can never forget that he died two months later.

As with everyone in a therapist's office, my maladaptive behavior stems from my childhood. Weekly, often nightly, my mother would attack me in various ways and for unconscionable reasons that will forever linger in the universe as proof that the mere presence of functioning ovaries does not make someone a mother. My mom was almost assuredly a borderline herself, unmitigated and irascible. She grew up in Texas, too—a state where public health is confined to the Second Amendment. Given the woefully poor resources that my mother was provided, she probably became the best version of herself that she could become. That said, she was a monster.

Her assaults could start at any geographic location on the planet, but they would always end with both of us in my room. This two-person performance was played on repeat for insanity and would always whittle its way down to the following scene: My mother, standing above me, the enormity of her shadow filling up more space than both of our persons combined. Me, sitting on my bed, my shoulders slumped in apparent shame and deference, my eyes cast down in forced penitence. There was a specific area of the carpet I would focus on, a constellation of stains seared forever into my memory in Kool-Aid pink. The more she hit me and the more she yelled, the deeper I would bury my fingernails into my skin, while I hugged myself tighter, as somehow that provided me the fortitude to not fight back.

Eventually it would end, and I would be left alone, still sitting on my bed. As soon as she would leave my room, the second she turned the right corner, I would examine my arms. The deeper the nail indentions, the more vindicated I felt. If there was blood? Excellent.

I'm not sure how other people happen upon anything as seemingly counterinstinctual as self-harm, but the release must be the same, regardless of how the behavior is learned. When I discovered that I could redirect my internal turmoil into an outlet that I could control—physical pain—it changed the game for me; it gave me a way to win.

Years went by. More years went by. I moved from Oklahoma to Texas to Tokyo to New York City. It didn't matter where I was or who my friends were; I was acutely aware that I was different and that something was wrong with me. People learned to hide the knives; jokes were made to make light of it. Clothes and bandages had to be worn over telltale scars.

A year after my father died, my mind began to crack open. Whatever it was that was different about me was now as visible as the scars on my arms. I felt like a turtle without a shell, or butter sliding off of a hot pancake. I would write in my journal about how unseasonably warm it was in New York, followed with, "I'm afraid to have a child, because I will kill it." These thoughts danced across the page in sloppy handwriting that is as unrecognizable to me as the words on the paper.

"I had a mental breakdown when I was walking to work today," I wrote in a letter to my dead father on November 2, 2011. "I couldn't stop crying. It was that hideous choking crying that everyone realizes is a complete loss of control. I hope that you were there. I was thinking of you. I wanted to cut myself. I still do. I was also thinking of jumping off of the Manhattan Bridge, too. I almost made a right where I needed to, and when I passed it, I stopped for a second to turn around. But then I thought I would probably just wimp out, and then I would be late to work. I feel like everything is slipping away again. I feel so alone here. I feel so, so alone. I feel sorry for myself, too."

A little over a month later, I poured a full bottle of children's strength Benadryl pills down my throat. Because what could possibly be a more convincing condemnation of life than overdosing on an over-the-counter antihistamine used for the temporary relief of seasonal allergies in four- to twelve-year-olds?

After a few days in a medical unit, I was transferred to the psychiatric ward at Lenox Hill. This was my first inpatient hospitalization, and it didn't take long for my smart Manhattan doctors to bless my forehead with the words "borderline personality disorder." It was weirdly purifying, comforting even. I was part of a classification of people with similar issues—not just a girl alone in the middle of the ocean trying to stay above water. For the first time, I had found hope.

As it was, my inpatient stay in Lenox Hill's eighth ward coincided splendidly with the holidays. We decorated cardboard gingerbread houses with candy and glued the pieces together with icing. On Christmas Day, we were visited by a Santa. He recited "The Night Before Christmas" with robust enthusiasm as we congregated around him in our hospital-issued sky-blue pants. That evening, we positioned ourselves slumber-party style on comfy couches for a televised broadcast of *The Sound of Music*.

Soon after, I was discharged and released onto the streets of the city. I was—as my then-boyfriend said shortly thereafter—"cured." It was lovely to think, and it was also entirely incorrect.

Later, I learned how atypical my experiences at Lenox Hill had been. At Bellevue, for example, I could never see the TV. This is because there was always the same scruffy googly-eyed enthusiast parked directly in front of it, blocking my view of the Brazilian Butt Lift, a thirty-minute advertisement played on repeat on a channel he almost always had it on.

Over the first half of the 2012 calendar year, I was hospitalized seven times for increasingly aggressive attempts at putting myself in a coma, giving myself seizures, or actual suicide. It didn't matter how long my inpatient stay was or whether it was a state-funded or privately funded institution; I would be involuntarily hospitalized again within two or three weeks. I was getting worse, not better, and none of my treatment teams could figure out why.

It took a while, and the revelatory breakthrough of "why" occurred independently of my clinicians' oversight and only as a follow-up to the final, seventh hospitalization. Apparently, I needed to thoroughly acquaint myself with every psychiatric ward in the city before I could reach enlightenment.

After a particularly visceral expulsion from the esteemed New York Presbyterian DBT outpatient program, I had told my therapist to call 911. Instead, she hung up on me.

Beyond the lack of professionalism, the recklessness she exhibited in this event cannot be overstated. New York Presbyterian had placed me under her supervision as part of my outpatient treatment plan after a legitimate suicide attempt less than a month prior. Beyond this, if having someone hang up on me had been in any way therapeutic, ever, I never would have gotten sick. And if my crisis safety plan could have been so concisely limited to the abrupt termination of a phone call, then there were plenty of individuals who would have been happy to take me up on that. For free.

Click.

Just as I cannot overstate her recklessness, I cannot overstate my reaction. I genuinely needed help, and this had been the first time I had reached out to a licensed professional instead of to a friend or boyfriend.

The only reason my eighth hospitalization didn't occur that afternoon? Fiery, raging pride. The desire to hurt myself was white-hot and excruciating, but so was my need to make sure that no one, especially *her*, could say I was too sick for outpatient treatment. Up until that point, I had taken a passive approach to my treatment. I did as I was told, did all of my homework, but the reins were always in the hands of my trained clinicians. But as I realized then, these clinicians were not infallible. If I was going to get out of the cycle of hospitalizations, I was going to do it on my own.

Earlier in this text, I used the analogy of a turtle without its shell. That day, I grew back my shell. I switched over to my own psychiatrist, took control of my medication, and refused to refer to myself as a borderline. And I definitely refused to call 911 or ask for professional help. If I overdosed, I would vomit into a bucket on the side of my bed. If I cut myself, I would put butterfly sutures on open wounds until they weren't open anymore. I got better because I said I would get better, and eventually I *did* get better, and it was as simple as that.

When I kicked my boyfriend's second-story apartment glass window, it was two years later. I was drunk and angry and therefore impervious to reality, such as gravity and physics. I fell into the window, passed out from shock, and woke up straddling the ledge with one leg partially dangling outside and the rest of it severed by a pane of broken glass. I remember trying to sit up, but my vision blurred to black with bright white lights in the center. "This is such crap," I said to myself. "This is so clearly the result of a lack of blood flow to my brain. I never want to hear anymore about this bright lights right before death bullshit, ever." And with that I lost consciousness again.

It took a nine-hour surgery and two additional surgeries later to save my foot. I used a walker for a long time, then crutches, then I was back on a walker, and then finally, just an orthopedic moon-boot shoe. A little over six months after the accident, I was able to put on two sneakers. I even have it on video, my first steps, the second time I learned how to walk.

So where am I now? Not cured, obviously. Although I had believed I had been, immediately prior to slicing my leg in half. I am, however, finally thrilled to be less enslaved by myself than I used to be. This is partially because I have stopped drinking, stopped smoking cigarettes, stopped ingesting things that give me anxiety, and no longer dabble in recreational drug use. Going along with this enterprising new behavior, I gave up an eating disorder, fueled by Adderall and excessive exercise, in favor of a reasonably healthy diet. Along with not being hungover, I start each day on sturdier ground than I ever did before.

The borderline thoughts and feelings are still there, though, hiding below a thin exterior. Just as I still have to resist the urge to smoke cigarettes, I also have to resist the urge to throw things, to dig my nails into my arms, or to hit people. I still fantasize about vindicating perceived slights by causing injuries to others, I still obsess over impossible hypotheticals, and—still—I have yet to look at a box cutter without imagining blood spilling down my limbs and the twisted, satisfying release I derive from that.

There are so many ways to elaborate upon how far I have come without really coming very far at all. BPD sucks; the silver linings aren't silver enough to paint any rosy pictures. There have been many instances where I have screamed out loud to a god that I don't necessarily believe in, begging him to save me by killing me, as I clawed at myself; also cursing him for the injustice of allowing me to be born at all.

It's amazing what a person can bounce back from when they have to. And it's even more amazing when a person bounces back stronger. We're not fighting burning buildings, at least not the kind people can see. But we're dealing with an uphill battle, and the only way we'll ever get to the top of the hill is if we keep walking.

I have seen and experienced hell. I have a deep indentation in my right lower leg that is less of an indentation than an absence of flesh. My toes are paralyzed because of my injury; I can never run again, and I have a permanent limp. I have a seven-inch Nile River gash descending vertically down my left wrist, and accompanying streams, creeks, and estuaries on either wrist. I have lost everything, been homeless, built myself back up from scratch, and lost it all again. Twice. All because of this thing called borderline personality disorder and what it has meant for me.

But if I can keep walking uphill, assiduously applying myself to improving my mental health, then I will continue to get better. I'm proud of myself for getting to where I am now and all on my own, and in spite of myself. It's not a "happily ever after" ending, per se, but the happy ending for this essay is that I'm alive, I have two feet, and as soon as I am done writing, I can press save and walk away.

Besides, the story isn't over yet.

And there's hope in that.

19. Treatment at Halliwick

My problems began in childhood and adolescence. My difficulties were overwhelming, especially with my mother, who continuously lied to me, from trivial things to major issues. I had a persistently difficult relationship with her, and I was frequently abused physically by her. She hit me until a late age in adolescence, and her look, with steely cold eyes when nasty, terrified me. I would binge-eat and also had bulimic episodes. Additionally, because my family had moved several times, during adolescence I struggled to make friends. The worst feeling was the intense anger. I had explosions in my head and mood swings frequently and "lost it" over very small things. I was hypersensitive, which made me impossible for my mother, just as she was impossible for me. My parents, in a strange way, loved me, yet my mother had no interest in my emotional distress. This was very destabilizing for me.

I have read about invalidation, and it made sense to me. Every time I said something about how I felt, my mother seemed to disallow it. I was supposed not to feel as I did. I always had to see things her way. This was the most sensitive area between us. I started eating excessively, so junk food was constantly hidden away from me. Eventually, I became overweight with bulimia.

By my late teens, I was self-harming regularly. I was triggered into self-harm and often, although I did not know it then, was very dissociated. I was able to work out that my complex relationship with my mother was a major trigger to my feelings. The emergency department staff members were quite nice to me when I took overdoses. I did not have bad experiences in the accident-and-emergency departments, although I know that some people who take frequent overdoses feel ill-treated. The kindness from the staff helped me feel looked after. I had safety there, yet I was so vulnerable. It had become a ritual for me to OD every time my mother was very nasty to me. I felt overwhelmed with emotional abuse and had deep feelings of hatred and anger, so that I did not think I could do anything else. My head felt like it would explode with so much noise. I was tormented about my weight, as I was overweight and it had led to some unpredictable bullying. I was a mess and needed treatment.

Going into a service for borderline personality disorder was frightening. However, after being rejected by so many services, it was a new, positive experience, although I was extremely distrustful. I often felt that I was not taken seriously, and one psychiatrist had been so dismissive of me that I trashed his office. Not surprisingly, he would not see me anymore and referred me to the Halliwick Personality Disorder Service at St. Ann's Hospital in London. At Halliwick, I got a firm diagnosis of BPD. Previous services had said they did not know how to help me, and I had been told I had depression.

Initially, I was taking overdoses regularly for reasons I did not understand, and my behavior was concerning to the whole team. I explored the triggers of my overdoses, initially, as we both agreed that this was endangering my life. I did not care, really, but the responsiveness that I received from K and the team made me begin to reexamine things. Trust and attachment were crucial here, to shift away from distrust and paranoia. My overdoses were strongly related to very painful feelings of rejection and invalidation (my feelings were never acknowledged, but trivialized). But so many things would undermine me that I was constantly in danger when with other people. But if I was on my own—by now I was living on my own—I felt lonely and needed someone. I had safety when alone but was so vulnerable. The lack of criticism about my behavior, and the sense that K could understand the necessity to overdose, was the thing that allowed me to choose another way. I realized that I felt more stable by taking overdoses, even though they could kill me. Everything was organized around me when I was on the ward, and I was back to familiarity. Because I trusted K, we agreed I would tell him, or someone from the team, when I started to feel like self-harming. The idea was to stop my feelings escalating out of control. The progress, for me, was having someone I could trust, someone who was stable and who grounded me well. I knew where I was. In therapy, the important bit was that I could tell K whatever was troubling me and when the urge to overdose started. I began to recognize the danger signs.

Most sessions, I slumped into the chair, my full body weight sinking with exhaustion. I remember vividly a look I got, which was "This must be so hard for you." Previous therapy elsewhere had not reached me. This was a funny therapy, using psychodynamic treatment, but it was being developed in the unit as mentalization based treatment. I had an individual session plus some group work.

In the individual sessions, I was frightened by how volatile I would feel. The initial sessions felt doable and gentle. We had to get to know each other. However, it was hard work. He seemed interested. I was distrustful.

Initially, I spoke about everything in a loud, chaotic way. At times, K would quiet me down and then ask me something difficult. However, I often struggled to answer, because I just did not know the answers. I cried often and felt it did not matter that I was unable to answer. I was demanding more and more of K's time, and I was becoming problematic and disrupting the therapy. This was dealt with compassionately but firmly. I met with the team, and we agreed on a plan for me to manage my constant demands. I would phone up regularly and ask for more time, even panic that I might take overdoses even though these had begun to decrease dramatically. We agreed that, outside therapy, I would speak to other team members about specific difficulties or needs. This had firm boundaries, too. Surprisingly, I never felt unheard or betrayed. It hurt sometimes, and I was encouraged to take my feelings back into the session. As time moved on, I managed my urges better, and I began to value the work tremendously. But at this point, I struggled to contain my feelings at times and demanded more attention. I kept trying to push the boundaries and wanting more, feeling that it wasn't ever enough. This was a turning point, where I realized I would always want more but could never get enough. I was able to work on this in the sessions, but then it happened, without warning: I started to think about K all the time. The attachment I had to him occupied my mind. I was very aware of my strong and alive feelings. When having thoughts about him, I wanted to see him. He helped me to find the point where I was satisfied and had enough to keep me going without demanding more and more. Looking back, I was bingeing on seeing him, because each day felt a long way from the next session.

It was by being taken seriously that I could talk and develop a sense of trust and stop my painful destructive behavior. It was not easy. I can choose life instead of trying to die.

However, the therapy was stormy too at times, because this sort of intensive interaction was frightening too. At times, K misunderstood a very small thing, and I would find that difficult to tolerate. I was attached. One particular session, we did some intensive work on my eating behavior, and I did feel safe to talk through what was happening. However, he said something that upset me, and I stormed out. He followed me to call me back in. I sat in the waiting room, furious. Other patients said K had come to ask me to go back in, so it must be serious. I took a few minutes and went back in. He had hit another painful spot of mine. I remember crying and telling him how much I hated the chaos. I had a breakthrough. I was able to start looking after myself. I think this was because I had chosen to go back in and not to leave.

Looking back, I made unreasonable demands out of desperation. The team was always respectful and took my demands seriously, but they specifically differentiated this from necessarily meeting my demands; for example, they would listen to my demand for more time and explore it but would not necessarily fulfill it. I was supported to keep working on the painful feelings and never made to feel bad. The good experience of having meaningful, validating experience at times felt bad. The good experience of being supported made me feel like a kid, at times, with a new toy.

One of my major problems had been binge eating. We started work on a food diary that I struggled to do. However, I was always told that honesty was important, so that they could help me. "If we don't know what's happening with your eating patterns, how can we help you?" It was hard talking about my eating, and it made me not want to do it. This was from my experience of being bullied and tormented for so long over my food. I have never really gotten over it all. As I sit here, writing, the nastiness and scathing comments I remember still make me feel bad. I was so angry; I felt so overwhelmed. Yet it continued for many years.

As I opened up, I started to appreciate the delicate, sensitive, and honest therapeutic relationship. Being sensitive, we worked around my needs. I was constantly pushed, but in a respectful way. The closeness in my attachment to K meant that, over time, the safety and trust was solid, and I therefore was able to start working harder to control the food and how I ate. The control was very emotive. I really wanted the control, yet I did not want to do anything that pleased my mother. It took the close safety of K to unravel the complexity, so that I could find my own dignity and strength.

Working on my eating disorder was hard. Regular weigh-ins with K and the dietitian. I got to a point where I felt safe and started controlling the chaotic food. The food-diary work was intensive and very painful. I was learning to eat normally and properly, and I was struggling with eating in a way that my mother would approve. This was an important issue for me. I had to take the risk to feel better through professionally guided behavioral changes. Negotiations, at times, were stormy; however, we all worked well as a team, and we never gave up.

Over time, I learned that I could enjoy a proper meal. I discovered I really enjoyed foods that I had never tried before, such as certain vegetables; however, I was very careful that my mother didn't know too much about my changes. I had to retain control over my feelings and food choices as much as possible. I valued the fact that at home I started to implement changes and in my fridge, once I had my own flat, were foods that I was happy about. It was a huge shift. My independence has come from having my own flat and autonomy over my fridge and kitchen. I kept going to the fridge to remind myself, "My choices, my life."

The hardest part of opening up and telling K how much I had been eating was a very painful reality check. However, he never undermined my efforts. We knew how complex it was.

Learning how to stop my self-abuse in eating was empowering for my own capabilities. I was then able to start saying no. It took a long time to work through. I had to gain some control over the food first and then grow stronger as I felt more stable. My mind was tormented, and the safety and warmth of working with K allowed me to reduce the intense feelings of my desire to self-destruct. I could say no to abusive behavior and comments on a more regular basis. There were still explosive interactions between me and my mother, but the stability of therapy was rock solid, and it felt safe.

The process of change in my eating then exposed many issues to work through, and I started to work on honesty. I had no idea what honesty meant, other than I had it with K, and I was honest with him and the team; that was a good place to be.

How could I trust and be honest in real, outside relationships?

The anger I had was allowed to diminish over time, as I felt less volatile. The validation that I got is what helped me to develop myself into a better person over time. However, it was taking a very long time.

The last stage of therapy was fast approaching, and I found the sessions very intensive as well as progressive. I was tackling other things, like what keeps me ill: the struggle with relationships, especially with my mother and family. The anger had simmered down over time, and that also allowed me to feel calmer within myself. Although my anger at her remained in a massive way, it felt manageable, within normal limits, and no longer dysfunctional. I had fewer explosions. Previously, rage was a huge issue for me. I had always believed my size reflected the size of my anger. As my weight stabilized, I was able to consider my behavior too. The mood swings were still distressing; however, I was less volatile. I worked hard at taking control of the rage, anger, weight, coping strategies, to avoid self-harm triggers: I had to be honest with myself and become a less dysfunctional person.

The last few months of therapy went very quickly. Although not recovered, I was considerably happier, less chaotic. The ending was very painful and moving. I put everything into this effort; things were improving.

20. Reasons

I spent years believing that if I tried harder, I could be different, better, normal. I saw most people around me handling life without crumbling at every onset of emotion and concluded that I was clearly doing something wrong. It took me years to realize there was a reason things were more difficult for me, but even at that point, I continued to believe that my failure to experience things normally was due to a flaw in my character and a lack of effort, as opposed to a medical condition.

Everything I feel is magnified, and my ability to rationalize those feelings or control my reactions to them is underdeveloped, which means that, most often, emotions hit me completely unbridled and take me by surprise. My thoughts take off in a whirlwind, trying to comprehend what is happening, but more often than not, they contribute to intensifying the emotions, and my body reacts immediately. This is what happens, no matter what I experience, positive or negative—fear, joy, excitement, anger, sadness. With positive emotions, it can feel like a blessing at first, like a drug, like being invincible, but it quickly becomes as distressing as anything negative. The intensity of what I am feeling is overwhelming; it is impossible to process all at once, and my reactions to it are extremely difficult to control. In the end, every type of emotion can be exhausting and feel like too much to bear. I spend every day feeling too much and trying to anticipate the next wave. I watch people keep an even keel and express their emotions in controlled social cues, while I struggle to hide the fact that every emotional reaction feels like a tidal wave. My rational mind actively tries to think through emotions, to decide whether the distress I am in is warranted, but my body reacts less logically. I find myself shaking or crying. Sometimes I have trouble breathing, or I feel dizzy or nauseous. Sometimes there is such an overload that I begin to dissociate, as my body attempts not to feel anything at all. I fill the rarer moments of what feels like lucidity with thoughts of self-loathing, blaming myself for my inability to change or to do better, convincing myself I'm a burden on those who love me. I can logically understand why suicide is not something a healthy mind can comprehend or process, but suicide is the thought that most often comes to mind when, year after year, this is the reality that follows me, no matter how far I run.

Some days, it isn't a desire to die but simply to hurt in a different way. "Changer le mal de place," as my mother would say in French. It means putting the pain in a different place. The pain can be so unbearable, it seems logical to purge it with more pain; I transfer it out of my body like bleeding out an illness. The angry scars on my forearms are a testament to this. It becomes a drug, a habit I fight every day. I have a habit of unscrewing the blades from pencil sharpeners and tucking one behind my iPhone case or in that tiny pocket on the front of a pair of jeans. Having one within reach makes me feel more at ease. When I pull the blade across my skin and see blood pouring into my hands, I know I am alive and able to process pain like a normal human. It is logical that I am hurting; physical pain is much more easily processed than emotional pain. I slice at my skin until my hands are red from the blood, and I pull my shirtsleeves back down, letting it feel wet against my skin and feeling the added pain of an open wound against cotton. I am an addict. I have sometimes excused myself from a party to take refuge in the bathroom and bleed out my demons, to carve some courage into my skin, in order to return with the happy facade of the fearless, fun-loving blonde. This kind of pain is logical. I have neatly packaged it in a way that makes sense. In these moments, I hold crimson pools of all my shortcomings and inadequacies, and I do not want to die; I want to feel alive.

From what I understand, most people's lives are a somewhat controlled oscillation between sadness and happiness. Both are to be expected, and both are manageable. Some losses or traumas are more than a person can handle, and in those moments, most anyone would break down, but for the majority of their days, most people feel content and stable. They experience sadness and happiness in a way that makes sense, but these words seem meaningless to me. I live on a greater scale, a spectrum of extremes, where control is an illusion found in blood, sweat, and tears, at the bottom of a pill bottle, on the blade of a knife, or halfway across the planet, as I try to outrun everything I feel. They are at each end of an always swaying pendulum and the constant rush of the waves I'm drowning in. This dichotomy of positive and negative emotions is both what keeps me alive and what keeps me in constant distress. Each end of the spectrum becomes the only thing I experience, all I can possibly comprehend, and all I remember. Happiness makes me feel like I will never know depression again, like I am no longer broken, and as long as I choose to feel this way, everything can stay perfect. That happiness is of a magnitude that is impossible not to crave, but the pain and the sadness can shatter it in a moment, and all of a sudden, I am inviting death in again. All of a sudden, there is no end to the darkness, no solution, and I forget what it feels like to feel joy or even to feel anything neutral. I do not think neutral is something I intrinsically understand. I just know pain, these excruciatingly beautiful moments that feel like the world will never be this perfect again, and dull, aching, drowning darkness. The pain cannot be endured without those moments of inescapable joy, and that joy requires me to give so wholly of myself that pain is inevitable. The highest highs and the lowest lows, yet they are so similar.

I rode an ATV around Mykonos, in Greece, once, my hair free in the wind and my iPod blaring, as whitewashed and blue-trimmed towns blurred by. I turned a corner and found myself at the top of a cliff watching the horizon turn a soft orangey pink and the sun set into the deep turquoise of the Mediterranean. I stopped. I stood on my ATV, turning the music even louder. I could have jumped off the edge of that cliff. I wanted to breathe in the pinks and oranges and smoke out every bad thought I'd ever had with these soft bright colors. In that moment, I was truly limitless, invulnerable. I laughed and reached up to the sky. I could do anything. I was everything I had ever wanted to be. I needed no one. *This isn't real.* A small part of me knew it, but I stared as if I would never have the chance to gaze upon a sunset again, as if I would never be this complete again. By the time the last ray of sunlight disappeared behind the horizon, I felt empty again.

I wonder sometimes how much of what I feel, and of the disorder I have, is based on broken memories and broken love, and how much of it is simply who I am and the way my brain functions. I so constantly feel it—whether I am at the southernmost tip of South Africa where two oceans meet, at the top of a mountain 4,321 meters above Uganda, or in an apartment not ten kilometers from where I grew up—I am led to believe part of it is inherently who I am. I feel it all, I feel it consistently, and I feel it too much. But someone once told me that I was like the sea: wild, full of spirit, and boundless. I couldn't tell you right now what that feels like, but I know I've felt it. I am like the sea. Boundless indeed. I conquer things. I race at a hundred miles per hour and accomplish more than others do in a lifetime. I am a thousand things, yet I am nothing at all.

You might think I would wonder sometimes what draws me to want to kill myself or hurt myself. In the moments before each suicide attempt, my heart is racing, but my mind is clear. The storm of feelings is pushed aside, because calm sets in: the peace of mind that I have beaten my demons and that I have found a way out. A healthy brain cannot relate to this. People often stare at my wrists. There is nothing ambiguous about those scars. I wear my insides carved into my outside. It can feel as if the ugliest parts of me are on display, and people, well, they stare. I may have adorned my body with tattoos that are meaningful to me, but these scars are pain that life has tattooed on me when I was too weak to exist: ladders of thin horizontal white scars from the times I tried to climb out of the depression and thick glossy lines of healed flesh from a moment when I was not strong enough to live up to the potential flowing through my veins and tried to drain them clean. I told myself, this time would work. I felt like a surgeon excising something malignant but finding out it had spread; focused on efficiency rather than death. So I tried harder. I searched three inches deep into my arm, feeling as if I had spent years fighting a storm and, if only the blood would flow freely, I could calm it. But I failed. Again.

These parts of my story are visible and unavoidable. People might notice my wrists and feel confounded or burned out by angsty stories of self-harm, and at first glance, my pain may seem cliché, but it certainly is not trite. This is my story, and it echoes that of so many other people. It is one of shame turned into a journey and an attempt to heal, shame that comes from the struggle to control this disorder and all that it does to the people around me. I often think of the fact that my mother will live the rest of her life with the memory of my lifeless body as the paramedics tried to shock life back into me, with the memory of her only daughter strapped to a hospital bed. Shame comes from the lack of understanding of so many people, of people who should know better. I remember a police officer's hands, down to his fingerprints in black and blue on my forearm after he tried to restrain me. I was fighting with everything I had to stop the people trying to save me, and all he could find to say was "Show's over, kid." His contempt and ignorance echoed in my head long after he had left the hospital.

So many times in my life I have heard lectures of "you're too pretty, you're too talented, you're too smart to want to die." But is that really what feeling good in your own skin is made of? What feeling connected to the universe and to life feels like? Living is not something everyone is born with. Some of us have to learn how to do it, over and over again. Practice makes perfect, but the pain and the overwhelming emotions always seem to bring me back to square one. As they say with so many other things, it comes in waves. Another cliché, but that's because waves are eternal and drowning is a horrible way to go.

With every suicide attempt, the choice is so decisive and logical that I cannot imagine any reason the people in my life would not understand. But still, they wonder what would draw me to want to end my life. It is really the opposite. Every day I ask myself why I want to live. And every day I have to find a reason. Some days I find several, and others just one. Some days, however, I find none at all. And on those days, I have to hope I will find one tomorrow.

21. Angry All the Time

On a late-summer evening in 2014, the Milwaukee Brewers were playing at home against the St. Louis Cardinals. Nothing special; like most professional baseball teams, they played against each other about a million times a year. Just another day at the office. But it was late in the game, and the home team had its star pitcher on the mound, a notorious hothead whose only job was to come in from the bullpen and get the last few outs of the game. The Brewers were leading six to two. It was the top of the ninth, and there were two outs. The Cardinals had two men on base (second and third, for those riveted to their seats), and the batter had a ball and a strike against him. The pitcher, with a reputation for being wound just a wee bit too tight, threw the ball, and the batter took a mighty swing. Bat and ball connected, but not hard, making for a weak pop fly to the outfield. The Brewers' left fielder barely had to move—the ball floated right to him, and he caught it easily. Piece of cake. Game over. Victory for the home team.

The Milwaukee players gathered in small groups on the field and in the dugout, congratulating, giving each other high fives, smiling. *Shucks, that was fun.* The St. Louis players hung their heads, the batter who popped out jogged off the field, and the runners on base (second and third, remember) trotted toward their dugout.

And then it happened. Or didn't happen, depending on whom you ask. The expression on the hotheaded pitcher's face, in an instant, turned from victory smile to puzzled look. Then just as quick, a scowl. Then came the shouting, the yelling, the teammates restraining him (and then each other). The benches emptied, and all the players (and coaches, trainers, etc.) came onto the field to argue, threaten, claim injustices, and so on.

What had happened was the runner (on second base, not third) was leaving the field when the game was over, taking the most direct path to his dugout (when you play 162 games in a season, you don't look for the long way to...anywhere). That direct path took him past the pitcher's mound, where—yes, you guessed it—Grumpy Pitcher was taking praise from a teammate for getting the final out of the game.

Condensed version: runner passes pitcher; pitcher thinks runner came too close to him, possibly brushing up against the sleeve of his shirt. *It had to be intentional. He probably said something, too. An insult. Yes, he must have insulted me. That rotten SOB. I'm going to kill him.* "Hey, you! Yeah, you. What's your *#@% problem?" And so on.

Video replay shows that the runner did not brush up against the pitcher, nor did he say anything to the pitcher. But the pitcher perceived that something had happened, read into it what he did, and reacted in anger, and it was off to the rodeo for him and everyone else around him.

Everyone in the stadium seemed stunned by the bizarre turn of events. They all knew it was the pitcher's fault, because that was the kind of guy he was. Something like this always happened. Some were constrained in their comments, because

they were broadcasters or players within earshot of reporters—
certain language just doesn't fly with advertisers—but they all
had some version of "jackass" to describe the pitcher. I saw the
video on the morning highlights the next day, and I just
laughed out loud. I thought, *That guy is so me!*

I saw many sides of myself in that pitcher: intense, serious,
flip-the-switch mood changes; instantly excited in victory,
even faster to go to scorched-earth rage when slighted (whether
real or, more often than not, imagined). And all the stunned
players, coaches, and managers made me think of all the
people I can affect around me. Quite often, I perceive something as happening, read something negative into it, and react
in anger, and it's off to the rodeo for me and everyone else
around me. My mood swings cut a wide swath.

I've had plenty of epiphanies with DBT—quite often, a
direct result of being forced to look at long-held beliefs (frequently lifelong beliefs), compare them to the *facts* of the situation (information stripped of emotion and judgment), and
then decide whether my original belief was, in fact, correct—a
humbling exercise because I'm usually wrong.

I guess there's never just one reason for anything, but at
the root of my years and years of misery and suffering prior to
DBT was the fact that my father hated me.

I grew up on a farm, but I had asthma and couldn't be
around animals or dusty fields or crops, which hardly made me
an asset when most farmers' primary reason for having children, especially boys, was to have labor for the farm. I was a
worthless only son and a great disappointment to my dad, I
believed with all my being. Every time I got in trouble for
something, every time he raised his voice at me or looked mad,

it was the same thought that ran through my mind: *He hates me. He wishes I were never born. I am a burden, a mistake. He despises me.*

Connected or coincidence, I'm not qualified to say, but I hated everything. I hated myself: I was ugly, I was stupid, I was worthless. I hated the world around me; everyone else had parents who loved them. I hated anyone and anything that resembled a close-knit family. A truck drives by with a "...& Sons Construction" sign on it. I walk into a store and everyone working in the place was a family member, and I felt worthless. I started to hate my father, too. I hated, I hated, and I got mad. All the time. I was eight years old.

By the time I was about twelve or thirteen, I was full of pent-up rage. My father: I wanted to make sure that I never had a kid who hated me as much as I hated my father, and so I made plans to get a vasectomy as soon I could find a doctor who would do the procedure. Sports was my outlet for energy and aggression, but I frequently went overboard. In baseball, I would knock over anyone in my path on the bases; in hockey, I hit everyone as hard as I could—on one occasion hitting a guy so hard that I got a concussion. But he got the worst of it; the game was delayed while he was helped off the ice. None of these outbursts on my part are worthy of praise; rather they're useful points of reference for me to acknowledge that anger and rage have been unhealthy emotions for a long time.

As an angry kid, as a young adult prone to episodes of out-of-proportion rage, and as a full-blown adult who no longer gets the free pass of youth, I've kicked things, thrown things, broken things, said awful things, burned every bridge at work, at school, in relationships, and so forth. Around 2002, I walked into the Bronx VA Hospital and met a wonderful psychiatrist who said she thought she could help me with DBT. She was right, and she turned out to be more than wonderful. Over the years, she has, time and time again, proven to be extremely smart (brilliant, in my opinion), insightful, and equally gifted with compassion and caring.

Once a week for about six months, we met on Friday afternoon and talked. I was angry; everything made me angry. My father hated me; my life was empty. I felt as though if I were in a stadium with eighty thousand people cheering, did it matter if I stood up and cheered? Would I make a difference? No, they were having fun, and I didn't make a difference. Who cared whether I participated in life? Nobody. Women were repulsed at the thought of me. I had no friends. My parents were dead, my sisters hated me, and I hated them. "I think I can help you," the doctor said at the end of our first meeting. I was kind of stunned, but it felt wonderful to hear her say that.

Down the hall, once a week for about six months, we met on Monday or Tuesday afternoon in a group format. *What are you looking at?* I thought, as the guy nearest me watched me try to straighten my notebook where I sat at the end of the table. *There are no square edges on a damn oval table.* "I'm pissed off all the time, and I hate my father, and he hated me," I managed to squeeze in when it was my turn to introduce myself to the group.

Over the weeks, I shared with the doctor examples of my father's hatred of me, reasons why he didn't care about me, and instances and events of how my anger and rage created problems for me in day-to-day life. Over these same weeks, down the hall, group therapy operated for the most part as a classroom to learn DBT and a laboratory to role-play and practice these new skills with other patients. I learned skills that would allow me to talk with someone whom I was unhappy with—as opposed to storming out of a room, doing or saying something that would likely lead to my never speaking with that person again. In role-play, I was shocked to learn that almost every time I recounted an event from the previous week that had enraged me, it was crystal clear to people that I was angry, but they had no idea what I was angry about. I perceived something bad, awful, or negative, but usually it wasn't something others saw as reasonable to be so angry about.

It started to crystallize for me. Slowly, but consistently. When I get into an emotional state, I tend to be wrong. The more emotional I get, the more wrong I tend to be.

On the last day of group therapy, our assignment was to come to class prepared to discuss radical acceptance. It had been the final lesson the week before, and we should each have had an example of our own to share. I came to class with no idea what my radical acceptance would be. But I was absolutely committed to coming with an open mind. The focus of my day was reflecting on my conversations with my doctor over the months of Fridays and with the DBT skills she had taught over the many Mondays or Tuesdays of group.

In one-on-one sessions, I was able to see that I was probably wrong in a lot of my assessments of my father's feelings toward me. When he yelled at me, was it possible that he was just talking to me the same way his father had talked to him? I'd never thought of that, but my doctor did, and I thought she had a point there. If he really hated me, would he have left me a token amount of money greater than what my siblings got in his will, which seemed to indicate he wished he had been able to give me some money when I went to college? Well, *probably not*, I felt was the honest answer. These insights didn't just give me pause on the specific question; they made me think about the larger picture, with the issue being discussed being more important—as an indicator of the larger picture—than whether I was right or wrong on the specific question.

At the same time, the cumulative effect of the DBT skills—I was learning weekly and practicing daily—was resulting in changed behavior and changed outcomes in my everyday life. It was clumsy, but I was making an effort to describe to someone a situation that was making me angry and expressing how the situation was making me feel and telling them what I wanted them to do or say in order for me to feel good or better about the situation—this, as opposed to a more scorched-earth pattern of profanity and unfixable relations.

The overall effect of six months of DBT was that I was less agitated, both in frequency and degree, than before. I found myself open to new things, new ways of thinking. When the doctor asked me to make a list of things I wanted, because I'd spent my life focused on what I hated and was mad about, I found that I wanted a lot of things. I put together three pages of things under a heading of I WANT I WANT I WANT.

When it was my turn, I reflected on everything I had thought about that day, the most impactful conversations in therapy, the most impactful skills I'd learned in class. What I said was, "My radical acceptance is that my father loved me and I love him."

22. From Numbness to Happiness

I remember growing up never feeling happy, and that was my normal. I truly haven't been anxiety-free, depression-free, or confident in regulating my emotions until just recently. I started DBT in October of 2011, after years and years of unproductive therapy. I wanted to go—I loved therapy—but I was still depressed, suicidal, and had started cutting. My therapist at the time told me that I was looking for attention. Even though my world quieted down when I cut, the overwhelming guilt, because of what my therapist had said to me, would take over. My life consisted of feelings of not being able to breathe, skin crawling with pricks and pins, and pain so deep that the only thing that could ever possibly relieve it was cutting myself; that's what made it all go away. But my life resulted in a vicious cycle of pain, mistakes, and cutting, then back to pain and mistakes again. I wanted it all to stop so badly, and then came DBT.

I remember my first DBT therapy session, and I was scared to death. Even though I had not made progress, I still was attached to my other therapist, and I felt loyal to her. By the end of the first two-hour DBT session, I felt as though this might be a good thing. I started to really look forward to my sessions with my DBT therapist. But even though I looked forward to them, I found I couldn't answer questions; I had never been asked to describe my feelings and thoughts. I had no idea what to say. I was always so emotionally numb—no feelings at all, just numb—and there were no other words to describe that.

Within the first year of DBT, the first year, I had already made more progress than I had with my other therapist. I still couldn't see how my life was going to be worth living. I had lost a job, I could barely pay my bills, and I was still cutting and had chronic suicidal thoughts and urges. I ended up in the hospital several times during my first two years in DBT, and those times seemed to set me back some in therapy because I had to admit I was still suicidal and was still cutting, which I hadn't told my DBT therapist for fear of disappointing her. There were many times I would not share things with her, because I didn't want her to think I was really sick or crazy. I figured that if I acted "okay," then she would think I was, and keep helping me, but the cutting and self-harm was still such a powerful relief for me: I could feel something, I could sleep, and I could breathe again when I cut.

There were so many tough sessions and very cruel words that I would sling at my DBT therapist, trying to get her to leave me because that's what always happened to me. I thought, "If I sabotage this, she will leave me, and then I won't have to know the hurt I always feel when someone leaves me and abandons me." I had perfected the art of sabotaging. All through my life, high school, college, family, and friends. To this day, I really have no friends from my past. I pushed them all far enough away that they couldn't take it anymore. Because of realizing all of this and finally beginning to really, truly trust my DBT therapist and open up to her, I learned how to stop sabotaging my work with her, and because of that, and because she taught me how to stay put, open, and honest, I now have four true, lifelong friends, who have stuck with me through my hospital stays, through my ups and downs, and also through my successes, which is a first in my lifetime!

I had some amazing breakthroughs in DBT. I learned that just because I dislike something doesn't mean I have to take it on and make it right. It means it *just is*, and *I can stand it*. Some things are just supposed to happen because they do happen. This seemed like such an easy concept, but I really believed that I had to fix things or make them fair or find a way to make them not happen at all. When I finally did get, really get, that things *are* because they just are, and that's the way things are supposed to be, I could finally smile inside. I remember having the biggest smile on my face; it was my first real sign of progress, the first concept I could really understand, feel, and get deep, deep down inside.

There were very difficult times throughout my four years in therapy, as well. My relationship with my therapist had been my first healthy relationship, and I had shared some very intimate details of my life with her, things I had never told anyone before. I told her I trusted her, but my heart would tell me, "Nope. They all leave. Everyone leaves; they all go away. Don't do it. She will leave too if you tell her who and what you really are." I think I truly believed she was going to give up on me every time I would say cruel things to her. So? I continued saying hurtful things to her with the hope that she wouldn't, alongside of the hope that she really would give up. That way, I could prove to myself that I was right and that everyone really does leave, so I could be right but still miserable. But she kept sticking with me; I really don't know why, but she always stuck with me. I finally learned and allowed myself to trust her. This meant I had to be 100 percent honest with everything, both to her and, even more importantly, to myself. I had to believe down deep in my heart that this was going to last; she wouldn't give up on me until I had what DBT encourages us to set as a goal: a life worth living!

She never ever gave up on me throughout my years with her, through all four stages in DBT. I was able to reduce my twice-a-week sessions to once a month. I even dropped everything I ever knew in my life and moved to a remote village in Alaska to teach native kids. I would never have done that in my years prior to DBT. My DBT therapist taught me to take chances, to put myself out there, because I am okay the way I am, now. DBT taught me that I *can* do my life, I can do this move to Alaska, and *I can, period*. Where I live now is extremely isolated, but I can stand it and be okay with myself. Never in my lifetime did I think I could ever do this. Before completing DBT, I couldn't stand to be by myself, ever. I cried night after night, because I was so lonely. Now, I've learned how to be okay with myself, wherever I am. I learned that my own company is better than anyone else's. I learned that I am a walking miracle.

I think now about how I used to be and cannot believe I am where I am, in only a little over four years. That may sound like a very long time to some, but—after two excruciatingly painful, dark, and seemingly endless decades of standard therapy, experiencing year after year after year with zero progress, then in only four-plus years to experience how to become okay inside with myself, how to be a human, how to feel normal levels of anxiety, depression, happiness, trust, confidence and love—this is, by definition, a miracle. A miracle? For me, that was an impossibility! Absolutely no way I was *ever* going to ever be happy. Happy? That was for everyone else, but never for me.

And now, here I am to say this: Yes, borderline personality disorder is frightening. It sounds scary, and it's a horrible thing to have to endure. But I can also say that BPD is treatable and can be overcome with patience, persistence, and a well-trained DBT therapist who truly cares. It is *so* possible to get through it, so don't quit. DBT not only saved my life; it gave me one. Technically, I no longer meet the criteria for BPD anymore. I still have some bouts with depression, but I can stand them, and I can get through it on my own. I do have a life worth living, and now I'm working on a life worth really loving.

23. Mosaic of a Fractured Self

Borderline personality disorder (BPD)—just the name creates fear, aggravation, and exasperation in the hearts of mental health professionals. In the heart of a borderline? Amidst the shattered pieces that lacerate, fracture, and compel, the emotions are akin to a volcanic eruption and just as disastrous. How can I tell you what it is like to be me, someone living with BPD, without you first understanding the reason I live with it?

I am a survivor of sibling incest, spanning a decade, in a family that valued males over females and included a mother with her own mental health issues—undiagnosed. I was born number five of six and the only girl. My two oldest siblings, one ten years older and one five years older, spent my first fifteen years sexually molesting me. My father was absent, due to working long hours providing for this family. My mother, the main disciplinarian, couldn't or wouldn't confront the abuse she witnessed and, instead, blamed me, scolded me, and slapped me for being "dirty." I have scattered and minimal memories of my childhood and actually of my whole life.

My psychiatrist, now in our eighteenth year of therapeutic relationship, still likes to ask the question, "How has your sleep been?" I may remember how I woke up that morning, and maybe even a little before, but the night before? A hole. One of many. I cannot make a timeline of my life. I cannot even remember whether I took my meds until I realize I feel the telltale signs of antidepressant withdrawal—an electrical-shock type of sensation in the head and suicidal thoughts becoming more prevalent.

What are suicidal thoughts like? Rebellious, comforting, and thoughts I like to keep to myself. Why? Because of other people's reactions to them. While I was serving churches as the pastor, one person I confided in admonished me profusely for not having enough faith to overcome suicidal thoughts—another person condemning me, rather than listening. It has taken years for my psychiatrist to sit back and do nothing while I talk about feelings of death. This is progress, since she used to rush me to a hospital "for my own good." Suicidal thoughts are not dangerous; suicidal actions are dangerous.

Memory problems are not limited to medication lapses; one of my daughters told me about being very angry with me because of something I said to her years ago that I have no memory of. I have three adult children and one child lost to miscarriage. Maybe that child was luckiest of all. My three children were born within three years' time. So young, so fragile, and so unfortunate to have me as their mother. But that is a story for another time.

What is it like to be a borderline? Lonely. Deep-space lonely, even when in a crowd. I want friends. I want someone to understand me. I want that bond that humans can have with one another but I have never had. People are untrustworthy. The only way I know to deal with people is out of sight, out of mind.

If you are in my life, you are in it and remembered, somewhat. If I see you on a regular basis, I will know your name and a lot about you. I will help you out in every way. To the extreme, actually, and then I will resent that you do not go to the extreme for me. You will ask me, "How are you?" But only once. And you will hear from me, "Fine." You will accept that, without question. Without even asking, "Really?" That is what I would ask. And I would wait for the real answer. I am very skilled at reading people. I read emotions like you read words. I had to read people to survive. I will know a lot about you, very quickly. You, however, will know very little about me. I am afraid to tell anyone how I am. Because I don't know. I am fluid, ever changing, and, at times, explosive. I can be scary to others and always to myself. I am intelligent, compassionate to the extreme, and have empathy to the point of feeling your pain in my bones.

I do not do well in the world. I cannot keep my mood from ever-changing without chemicals, prescribed chemicals. I feel the ones I am using now are not enough. What is it like to be a borderline? To be on the border of sanity and insanity, reality and unreality? It is a precarious place to be.

I have worked at many careers. My résumé lists a myriad of employers, longest being the church and the VA medical center where I currently work. Serving as pastor in the church allows for normal compartmentalizing, which also is part of the borderline personality disorder. The pastor is an approachable enigma. People come to the pastor for confessional, spiritual advice, biblical instruction, and comfort, and to mark the defining moments of life and death. The pastor knows everything about the people in the church. The people need never know much about the pastor. This was a perfect fit for my mistrust of people and reticence to talk about myself. After all, what was I going to say? I was sexually abused by two older brothers for fifteen years, have no idea what emotion I feel at any given time, and think about the peace of death often.

Giving out personal information would lead to giving out feelings and what was really going on inside my head. I am always afraid that if anyone knew what was going on in my head, they would run away as fast as possible, probably scream- ing. In my head are thoughts of: *I am so lonely—won't someone be my friend? Stay away! Come closer. I don't trust you. Why don't you help me? No one cares. I might as well kill myself. I have obligations, I can't kill myself.* I want so desperately to be loved, accepted, by the family that abused me and made me invisible. I hope for something I cannot have, as this family is too dys- functional for change without therapy—they don't believe they are the crazy ones.

24. Riding the Waves

What does it mean to be borderline? What can we learn from a borderline? Borderlines are people too. They experience the world in an amplified way. Borderlines like me have ups and downs that are just a little more extreme than the ordinary person. They live from chaos to chaos and do not understand what it's like to go through life without constant pain and sorrow.

I went through life with a constant desire to die. I wanted to make the pain go away, but I did not actually want to die. I did not know how to communicate my needs and wants, so I acted them out in hopes of getting my needs met. I used repetitive sayings like "I can't do this," "I can't take this anymore," "I can't cope," and "I just want to die."

I tried to kill myself in so many different ways, but I am still alive. Something deep inside kept me alive. I don't know how, but for fifteen years I found myself contemplating my life and death.

I met a wonderful psychiatrist six years ago, whom I learned to trust, and she taught me how to feel without getting overwhelmed. She taught me that I would survive feeling and that emotions come and go like waves in the sea. They do pass, they do subside, and you do survive the ride of the wave. My psychiatrist taught me to trust and accepted me and allowed me to see that, regardless of what I did, she wouldn't leave me. She taught me to find balance in life and not to overload myself with busyness. The phrase I borrowed from her and integrated into my life is "Just because I can doesn't mean I have to." This phrase has allowed me to pick and choose what I fill my time with.

What Marsha Linehan states is that a borderline needs to create a life worth living. That life can be different for every person. It's a life that is right for you, beyond the chaos. For me, it was finding the love of my life and understanding and accepting that he loves me, just the way I am, and that he will never leave me. It was finding a job that followed my passions—a job that was fulfilling and allowed me to use my voice. It took many years before I could verbalize what I was feeling. My psychiatrist helped me find my voice. Finding my voice allowed me to become my own advocate and speak out for other people.

Taking charge of my own recovery was a step in the right direction. This means working with your psychiatrist and figuring out what your triggers are and what the best distraction and coping mechanisms are for you. Yes, it is good to come up with lists of skills, but will they ultimately work for you? This is where I was letting others tell me what would work for me when I needed to experiment and search inside myself to figure out how I could best help myself. You are ultimately your own expert. Yes, doctors and nurses can give suggestions and tools, but you have to put them into practice.

This is where fear and failure lurked within me. I was too afraid to try anything, because I wanted everything to be perfect, and this is where the black-and-white thinking emerged. I would either do something right or not do it at all.

I experienced all the faulty thinking that cognitive behavioral therapy states. It is really quite unbelievable that someone could actually have such negative thoughts, but I did. I was stuck in negativity. Life was miserable.

Life lacked meaning and purpose. It was depressing. I used to spend birthdays and major holidays in the hospital because I never wanted to start a new year, a new birthday, being the way I was. I was hopeless.

I was classified as a VIP at the hospital because I attended it so frequently. All the staff knew me. I was chronically suicidal and had chronic suicidal ideations. Life lacked meaning. Life was chaos.

Despite being hopeless and chronically suicidal, I was successful in the area of education. I obtained a degree and two certificates. I loved to learn and to challenge myself academically. I have a lot of head knowledge, but putting knowledge into practice and following through with a job was not possible. I drifted from job to job. I now know that I cannot do full-time work, and that is okay with me. I am learning my limits and how much work is too much. I am and probably will remain on disability for the rest of my life. I am okay with that. I do what I can, when I can. I try to live life in the moment, knowing that I may crash at any time. The unknown is difficult, but I try to keep my head above the water and swim or float. Sometimes I kick and scream, but I always keep swimming.

It is possible to be borderline and live a fulfilling life. I wish I had never received the diagnosis, I wish life would be easier, but I am coming to terms with my life. I only have one life to live. I might as well live the best possible life I can.

The best piece of advice I can give to a recently diagnosed borderline is to never give up; even when it seems like there is no light at the end of the tunnel, things do get better even if you can't see it. There will be storms and valleys, and you will have to climb out and stand strong, but it is worth it. Listen to your doctors and nurses; communicate your needs and feelings, even if you think they are off the wall or you think no one will understand.

Accepting and learning as much as you can about the diagnosis is key. Don't become defensive and bitter and hopeless because of the diagnosis. You can recover from borderline personality disorder. Life can be worth living, and it can be filled with hope. It is a process, not about the final result; it is about the journey, not the destination.

I had a dream once, a dream about crossing the border into wellness. I was in the country of sickness, and I illegally crossed the border into wellness without my passport. I found myself in the country of wellness as a stranger, like someone who did not belong there. So I went back across the border of sickness and went back to my old place and found that someone had already moved into my old place. I did not recognize it. I did not belong there anymore. So I found my passport and went back into the country of wellness and started my new life. This was foreign to me. I did not know where to start, how to be "normal," how to live beyond the chaos of sickness. It was like starting from scratch.

It took me two years before I felt like I belonged in the country of wellness. I still sometimes cross back into the country of sickness. My visits are less frequent and not as long now.

Afterword

Each of these stories gives a compelling picture of the subjective pain of having borderline personality disorder and the tortured pathways toward recovery that each individual has endured or—often enough—is still in the process of achieving.

One of the major themes in these accounts is that the diagnosis of BPD was a major turning point. Whether the initial diagnosis caused shame, revulsion, or doubt, all of these authors note that the BPD diagnosis eventually became an understandable mirror on themselves, which had powerfully positive effects. It reassured them that they were not alien, that others suffered similarly, and that they might find themselves understandable. It gave them information about the disorder's significant heritability. This diminished their self-loathing, by recasting their problems into a temperamental disposition for which they were not wholly responsible, while at the same time reducing the criticism and blame from their families or from others.

Above all, the diagnosis of BPD gave these individuals hope; they learned that those afflicted with this condition usually get better and there are effective treatments available. Both of these messages often contrasted with their previous experience, in which mental health professionals had given them other diagnoses (usually depression, bipolar disorder, or PTSD) for which they'd received ineffective and sometimes debilitating treatments, usually involving multiple medications. The message that accompanied these other diagnoses often meant that their recovery depended upon medication. The message that accompanied the BPD diagnosis was that their recovery depended on their learning to take control of their life. Many clinicians still fear that this message of personal accountability will only cause anger or shame. That response can happen, and in a few instances here it initially did. This does not occur, however, when patients have become as despairing about their future, in the face of multiple past treatment failures, as the majority of contributors to this book were. Many describe observing their peers moving on to productive lives while they were stuck in an intractable struggle with their limitations. For them, the borderline diagnosis uniformly awakened desperately needed hope.

The treatments received were heterogeneous, and varied. The most common was dialectical behavior therapy, reflecting its place as BPD's most widely available evidence-based treatment. But there were also examples of those who received transference focused psychotherapy and mentalization based therapy, two other widely recognized evidence-based treatments. Still, for the most part, few who entered into any of these evidence-based treatments then maintained a course that fits the standards of continuity and adherence used in research trials. This offers a valuable insight into real-world practices, where evidence-based treatments are often interrupted, modalities change, and resources are inconsistently available. Often these changes are caused by vicissitudes in the patient's motivations and life circumstances as much as by variations in the treaters' time, health, and usefulness. Such departures from the optimal protocol for participation in evidence-based treatments didn't prevent their being of value.

It bears noting that for some contributors the pathway to recovery didn't include exposure to any evidence-based therapy. They represent what the vast majority of people with BPD experience. There are only about fifteen to twenty thousand clinicians trained in evidence-based treatments, while the number of BPD patients in the United States is in the multiple millions. Yet most of these will also go on to sustained recoveries.

Whether the treatment received was evidence-based, intermittent, or not very consequential, what comes through is the stubborn and often unexpected resiliency and determination within these accounts. Time after time, I was impressed that these patients did not withdraw, did not commit suicide, and didn't give up their resolve to overcome their problems. I had thought that "good outcomes" for many BPD patients involved avoidance, such as learning to not expose themselves to the interpersonal triggers that figured so prominently in their younger years. That may sometimes be true, but these accounts are testimonials to those whose recovery involves a persistent, albeit painful, struggle to attain socially active and interpersonally satisfactory lives.

These patients are a selective sample. They were each invited to write accounts of their recovery from BPD in part because they remain in contact with their treaters. They accepted, in part, because they are articulate and confident enough to undertake this task. In some instances, a truly good recovery, meaning a productive social role and stable partnerships, has been achieved. We know that such outcomes are found in about 25 to 33 percent of BPD patients in ten years and as many as 60 percent by sixteen years. Such outcomes are underrepresented in these accounts. The obvious reason for this is that the patients who wrote these accounts were recruited from sites where they were still immersed in active treatments. What we see is more a picture of the turbulent processes of changes that are still underway.

I have mixed responses to this biased portrait. I am glad that the contributors conveyed their inner pain and their uncertainty about where their lives would end up. The surprising findings about BPD symptom remission—10 percent by six months, 20 percent by one year, 50 percent by four years, and 85 percent by ten years—don't convey that such victories are hard fought, fraught with crises, and often precarious. Having noted that the personal accounts collected in this book are often marked by resilience and a persisting hope for fully satisfactory lives, there is reason to think that many of these contributors will actualize their hope by finding socially rewarding activities that initiate self-perpetuating and self-enhancing cycles toward health.

These accounts uniformly bear witness to the varied processes by which such gains are achieved. That, I think, is this book's most important contribution. Readers with borderline personality disorder, those who love them, and the mental health professionals who treat them will doubtless take this lesson home and share my appreciation for these patients having made this lesson clear.

—John

Acknowledgments

The editors would like to thank the twenty-four authors for their dedication to this project. Their honesty in sharing their journeys made this anthology possible, creating a book that is the first of its kind and helping to demystify and destigmatize borderline personality disorder.

We would also like to thank the National Education Alliance for Borderline Personality Disorder (NEA.BPD) for access to site visitors. Without the organization's website, borderlinepersonalitydisorder.com, and its high ranking on Google, the worldwide announcement for the book would not have had the global presence for submission recruitment.

Great appreciation also to Dr. Richard J. Konet for his editorial support and objective perspective on what readers might find valuable.

Notes

1   The disorder, characterized by intense emotions, self-harming acts, and stormy interpersonal relationships, was officially recognized in 1980 and given the name "borderline personality disorder." It was thought to occur on the border between psychotic and neurotic behavior. This is no longer considered a relevant analysis, and the term itself, with its stigmatizing negative associations, has made diagnosing BPD problematic. The complex symptoms of the disorder often make patients difficult to treat and therefore may evoke feelings of anger and frustration in professionals trying to help, with the result that many professionals are often unwilling to make the diagnosis or treat people with these symptoms. These problems have been aggravated by the lack of appropriate insurance coverage for the extended psychosocial treatments that BPD usually requires. Nevertheless, there has been much progress and success in the past twenty-five years in the understanding of and specialized treatment for BPD. It is, in fact, a diagnosis that has a lot of hope for recovery. For more information, go to the McLean Hospital website (http://www.mcleanhospital.org), the National Alliance on Mental Illness website (http://www.nami.org), or the American Psychiatric Association website (http://www.apa.org).

2   *DSM* is shorthand for the *Diagnostic and Statistical Manual of Mental Disorders*, the standard classification of mental disorders used by mental health professionals in the United States. It is intended to be applicable in a wide array of contexts and used by clinicians and researchers of many different orientations (e.g., biological, psychodynamic, cognitive, behavioral, interpersonal, family/systems). The title of chapter 3 refers to the *DSM-5*, the most recent edition, which was published in 2013.

John G. Gunderson, MD, is professor of psychiatry at Harvard Medical School. At McLean Hospital, he is director of the Borderline Center's clinical, training, and research programs. Gunderson is widely recognized as the father of the borderline diagnosis. He is responsible for seminal research on the diagnosis, its course, its origins, and its treatment. These contributions have always been anchored within his role as a clinician whose practices are practical and compassionate.

Perry D. Hoffman, PhD, is president and cofounder of the National Education Alliance for Borderline Personality Disorder (NEA-BPD). Hoffman has several grants from the National Institute of Mental Health (NIMH) with a focus on families. She has coordinated over sixty conferences on the disorder, and is codesigner of the twelve-week psychoeducation course, Family Connections™, available in seventeen countries. In 2011, the National Alliance on Mental Illness (NAMI) awarded Hoffman the Excellence in Community Mental Health Award. To find out more, visit www.border linepersonalitydisorder.com.

Brandon Marshall is a three-time NFL Pro Bowler and All-Pro player. In 2006, he was drafted by the Denver Broncos, and in 2009, he set the all-time NFL record for receptions in a single game. In 2012, Brandon was traded to the Chicago Bears. Despite his success, Brandon felt controlled by his emotions. After years of ineffective therapy, he entered treatment at McLean Hospital, where he was finally diagnosed with borderline personality disorder (BPD), and learned the skills necessary to deal with his moods and emotions. He continues to use these tools today.

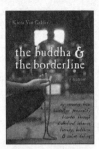
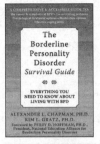

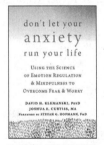

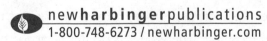